Hawks Rest

Hawks Rest

A Season in the Remote Heart of Yellowstone

GARY FERGUSON

NATIONAL GEOGRAPHIC
ADVENTURE PRESS
WASHINGTON, D.C.

Hawks Rest

Published by the National Geographic Society

Text copyright © 2003 Gary Ferguson
Map copyright © 2003 National Geographic Society

Parts of chapter 1 first appeared in *Big Sky Journal* 5 (summer 1998): 84-94. © 1998 Gary Ferguson

Printed in the U.S.A.
Design by Melissa Farris

Library of Congress Cataloging-in-Publication Data

Ferguson, Gary, 1956-.
  Hawks rest : a season in the remote heart of Yellowstone / Gary Ferguson.
    p.cm.
  ISBN 0-7922-6891-1 (pbk.)
    1. Yellowstone National Park—Description and travel. 2. Natural history—Yellowstone National Park. 3. Summer—Yellowstone National Park. 4. Ferguson, Gary, 1956- 5. Yellowstone National Park—Biography. I. Title.

F722.F475 2003
917.87'5204—dc21   2003042149

One of the world's largest nonprofit scientific and educational organizations, the National Geographic Society was founded in 1888 "for the increase and diffusion of geographic knowledge." Fulfilling this mission, the Society educates and inspires millions every day through its magazines, books, television programs, videos, maps and atlases, research grants, the National Geographic Bee, teacher workshops, and innovative classroom materials.

The Society is supported through membership dues, charitable gifts, and income from the sale of its educational products. This support is vital to National Geographic's mission to increase global understanding and promote conservation of our planet through exploration, research, and education.

For more information, please call 1-800-NGS LINE (647-5463) or write to the following address:
National Geographic Society
1145 17th Street N.W.
Washington, D.C. 20036-4688 U.S.A.

Visit the Society's Web site at www.nationalgeographic.com.

Contents

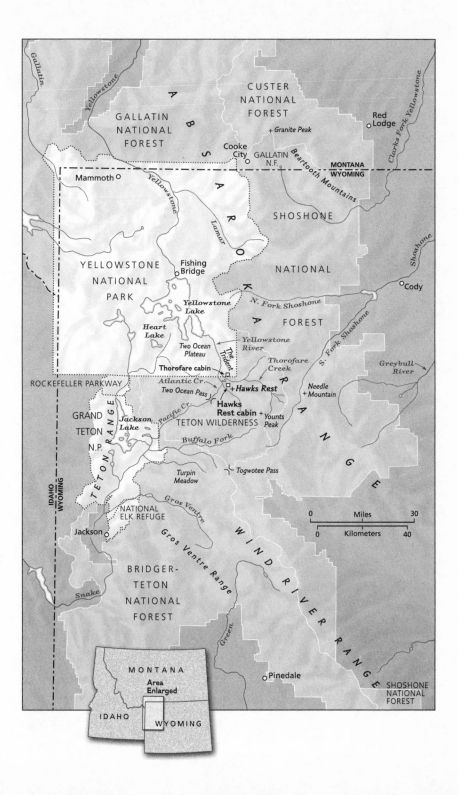

GALLATIN
Gallatin
Yellowstone

CUSTER
NATIONAL
FOREST

Red
Lodge

GALLATIN
NATIONAL
FOREST

A
B
S
A
R
O
K
A

+ Granite Peak

Clarks Fork Yellowstone

Cooke
City

GALLATIN
N.F.

MONTANA
WYOMING

Mammoth

Yellowstone

SHOSHONE

Beartooth Mountains

Lamar

NATIONAL

Shoshone

YELLOWSTONE
NATIONAL
PARK

Fishing
Bridge

N. Fork Shoshone

FOREST

Cody

Yellowstone
Lake

Heart
Lake

S. Fork Shoshone

Two Ocean
Plateau

Yellowstone
River

Greybull
River

The Trident

Thorofare
Creek

Thorofare cabin

ROCKEFELLER PARKWAY

Atlantic Cr.

+Hawks Rest

Needle
+ Mountain

Two Ocean Pass

TETON RANGE

GRAND
TETON
N.P.

Jackson
Lake

Pacific Cr.

Hawks
Rest cabin +

TETON WILDERNESS

+ Younts
Peak

R
A
N
G
E

Buffalo Fork

Togwotee Pass

Turpin
Meadow

NATIONAL
ELK REFUGE

Gros Ventre

W
I
N
D

Jackson

Gros Ventre Range

R
I
V
E
R

Snake

BRIDGER-
TETON
NATIONAL
FOREST

Green

R
A
N
G
E

IDAHO
WYOMING

| 0 | Miles | 30 |
| 0 | Kilometers | 40 |

Pinedale

SHOSHONE
NATIONAL
FOREST

MONTANA

Area
Enlarged

IDAHO

WYOMING

For LaVoy

M Y FINAL MORNING IN THE WILDERNESS, and it comes on the cold, bright spine of autumn. Mid-September, when beauty and death are joined at the hip, storming across the high country and filling the swales of the northern Rockies until the days seem too small to hold them. Thick, warm afternoons followed by frigid nights. Not a single morning breaks without the edges of streams and rivers being rimmed with ice—the upper Yellowstone, Thorofare, and Fall Creeks, the South Fork of the Shoshone; long before dawn, fireweed and lupine, gooseberry and harebell sag with frost. So too does ice form in cracks in the rocks, popping chunks of breccia off mountain faces. And then the wind, by noon full of bristle, stinging the tundra, cracking loose lodgepole pines burned in the 1988 fires, felling them in loud shots like the sound of the hunters' guns.

The days are swelled with signs of going. Canada geese honk and strut up and down the canyons of the South Fork, restless and quick to flush; songbirds and hawks, a few here and a couple dozen there, slip southward on some unknown signal, leaving the rest of us to nearly empty skies. In the mountain valleys to the west elk are massing, the bulls bugling and snorting, restless with the fever of the rut. In the wake of the first big snows they'll come pouring out of Yellowstone by the thousands. Some will head south, making for the National Elk Refuge near Jackson, or feeding grounds in the Gros Ventre Range. Others will turn east—traveling in my footsteps, as I've been traveling in theirs—moving up Thorofare Creek and over the divide into the South Fork, up the sheer western flank of Needle Mountain and on to the windswept valleys of the Greybull River. One of the longest migrations in the Rockies.

Over the course of the summer dozens of visitors asked me what I missed, what I craved most living in a patrol cabin for 11 weeks in the wilds of greater Yellowstone far from the drone and clatter of engines and fax machines and phones. I never managed much of an answer. Even now, on the brink of my return, it's nearly impossible to slip out of the present—as if the Absarokas were charmed, demanding always full attention, causing travelers to nearly forget who they were in that other world. Part of the spell comes from overwhelming beauty—great platefuls of it, full of wobble and swoon. It comes too from the fact that in every month are sharp squalls of snow and ice crashing across the high country, and in the heart of a great many summer afternoons lightning literally buzzing in the rocks. And then of course there's the grizzly, out in force now, charging about in that fiery state biologists refer to as hyperphagia, a kind of eating frenzy that begins each fall before the onset of denning. The fever may be even more intense this season given that one of the bears' favorite foods, the nuts of the whitebark pine, are in short supply, the result of drought and a tenacious, widespread disease known as blister rust; evidence of the infestation is everywhere, miles of brown branches smeared across the shoulders of the mountains.

In truth there's almost no end to the ferocity of this place, a wildness that tugs and shapes everyone who spends any amount of time here, on occasion wrenching them into something bigger than life itself. Even the names of some of the regulars make them sound like mystics, superheroes: Lone Eagle Woman from Wyoming, for example, who for the past 20 years has been wandering alone each summer across the high reaches of the Absarokas—as much at ease sleeping in these far-flung crannies as most people would be wrapped in their childhood beds. Or Yellowstone park ranger Bob "Action" Jackson, growing more famous by the month—in part for his battle with outfitters over the illegal use of salt to draw elk across the park's south boundary and, at the same time, for his fight with a Park Service that can no longer abide his provocative ways. And then there's that certain bible-thumping, gunslinging, illegal outfitter whose name is rarely mentioned at all, a feral and dangerous sort—out there long after the season has ended in the worst of mountain weather, going about the business of, as he puts it, hunting for God.

Grizzly bears and bouts of brutal weather aside, most people would probably imagine this place, the most remote in the lower 48 states, to be largely untroubled, unruffled, serene. I'd thought so too, coming here in large part to do the work of a naturalist: Record bear activity; make notes on the comings and goings of the Delta wolf pack; take the chance to explore the rise of new forests from the ashes of old burns; appraise populations of everything from white pelicans to eagles, moose to cutthroat trout; gauge the swell of berries in the lowland woods, rootstalks on the tundra. Not that I expected complete seclusion. It seemed a safe bet, though, that the roar of the land would be more than loud enough to overwhelm the comings and goings of humans. And yet there were simply too many of them, sometimes hundreds in a given week, flush with tents and lanterns and dogs, with long strings of horses and mules.

But beyond sheer numbers, I'm leaving today having come to know this vast twist of peaks and valleys as much as a kind of sanatorium for the disenfranchised, a way station for men riding and hiding, spring through fall, to escape whatever curses they imagine hovering in the culture at large. In these upper meadows of the Yellowstone is testosterone enough to light the woods on fire. Wanna-be cowboys roam the highlands by the dozen, each with at least one gun on his hip—angry, hating wolves and the government that reintroduced them. And more conspicuous still, an outlandish strain of outfitter, swaggering down these dusty trails and thumbing his nose at authority, living a kind of desperado fantasy that seems more appropriate to the 19th century than the 21st. "This is a lawless place," a veteran trip leader told a young Forest Service worker this summer about the outfitters in the area, comparing the place to the days of cattle rustlers in old Wyoming. "If I were you I'd consider a career in law enforcement. One day somebody's going to get hurt or killed back here and all hell will break loose."

IN THE 1840S there was an argument being made by nationalists eager to settle the more remote places of the American West: Without the gentling hand of civilization, they said, people would spin off, unleash all sorts of peculiar and unholy behaviors. Maybe so. Yet at the same time the vast majority of Native Americans thought it perfectly normal for beauty and craziness to stand together like this, arm and arm—two sides of the same leaf. Which may be closer to the truth. Or at least the truth as it shows itself here, in this far northwest corner of Wyoming, on the ragged edges of the Great Divide.

CHAPTER ONE

*P*OET JANE HIRSHFIELD ONCE REMARKED THAT
when it came to personal callings, hers was best described
as a struggle to match her life to a suitable landscape. Just my
luck, I guess, that my own hankerings would lead me to a slice
of high country roosting on a latitude halfway to the North Pole.
In a town where kids hunt Easter eggs in drifts of snow, where
girls head off to senior prom bedecked in strapless dresses and
Sorrell boots. Yet what summer in these mountains lacks in
duration it makes up for in heart, as bright and full of twitch as
a young boy's dreams. Evidence of what over a century ago
author Helen Hunt Jackson—also writing about summer in the
Rockies—described as "the great and tender law of compensation."
For ten glorious weeks, eleven in a good year, the days are
wrapped in the kind of warmth that pops leaves and melts
snow, that by some fine and murky sleight of hand manages to
soften time itself. In the way a suburbanite might set his clock
to the neighbor who steps out in his fuzzy slippers each day to

retrieve the morning paper, June through August spins on a wheel of blooms and berries, fur and feathers. Rising in the dawn are clatters of geese and the trill of dippers, and with twilight the woozy swoop of nighthawks. In early June whitetail fawns are napping among wild roses at the edges of the cottonwoods, while clusters of moose are beginning their summer rounds of the neighborhoods—enthralling some of the neighbors, scaring others half to death.

As the curtain goes up on all this drama I do my best to stay put—park myself behind the house in a tiny meadow of clover and dandelion and timothy, peel off my shoes and plant my toes in the dirt like so many onions. But it never lasts. Around mid-June my mind begins slipping away, drifting from the breakfast table out the door and across the aspen woods, climbing through the lodgepole and Douglas-fir hanging from the face of Mount Maurice, Town Mountain, the lip of Silver Run Plateau. One minute I'm eating toast, and the next I'm daydreaming at 10,000 feet, adrift on any of several sprawling plates of tundra that flow out of the heart of the Beartooths like the fingers of a hand, high and cold enough to coddle the shards of winter until long after the Fourth of July. And so it goes, day after day, until there's nothing left to do but make for the mountains.

This is no stray burp of granite rising out of the beet fields of northern Wyoming, only to sputter out on the banks of the Yellowstone. The Beartooths are only the beginning, the first chapter in a nine-million-acre epic known as greater Yellowstone, stretching from Livingston, Montana south past Jackson, Wyoming, Absarokee to Afton. A place that, with the return of the wolf, is in possession of its full plate of historic species, forming what biologists often call the largest intact ecosystem in the temperate world. A land of avalanches and rockslides, windstorms and wildfires and ice.

These lands, in turn, are at the same time locked to other places of intrigue: uplands dropping onto quiet runs of winter range—those, in turn, tumbling onto sage-covered plains. In truth it's the whole of it, including places way beyond what's needed merely to cradle the comings and goings of bison and pronghorn and wolves, that has for so long informed our dreams of the intermountain West. Humbling, crushing expanses of terrain. The kind of unfettered spans that led many 19th-century writers to say there was just too much of it. Even today, longtime residents fashion their mental charts of the country not so much from towns or highways, but from scattered notions of peaks and rivers and canyons, from massive promontories blasted by the wind. Our sense of place is not driven as much by specific historical events as by the shiver of a vague but powerful story line—the unwavering notion that life west of the 100th meridian is danced by land without end.

Over the years a few doodling geographers got it into their heads to chart the most remote places left in the continental United States. To no one's surprise the lists have been full of places in the West. The Frank Church–River of No Return Wilderness in Idaho. A lonesome toss of desert in southern Nevada. But the most remote spot of all is said to be right here in the northern Rockies, in the extreme southeast corner of Yellowstone National Park, in a place called the Thorofare. But with this news comes a catch, a jolt. Out of the million square miles of basin, range, peaks, and prairies that compose the interior West, the farthest it's possible to be from a road is a trifling

28 miles. One very long day's walk. It's not that we've lost our wild places. Rather that they no longer spill into unbroken quarters. Preserves that had been at the heart of vast, unfettered sprawls of land are for the most part now turning into islands. The rambling canvases of the West—places that were long the favorites for plastering our wildest, most eclectic dreams—have shrunk to something more comprehendible. If Freud was right to say that runs of unkempt nature serve the culture not unlike fantasy serves individuals, then our imaginations have surely become more tightly reined—walking, where once they ran.

When land preservation took wing in the last half of the 19th century, movements such as the effort to create Yellowstone National Park were thought to be fiercely patriotic. Congress itself got into the act in myriad ways, including securing as its first landscape painting for the U.S. Capitol a magnificent oil of the Yellowstone Rockies by Thomas Moran, bought for the astonishing sum of $10,000—a move fueled by the notion that such art was nothing less than a wellspring of nationalism. "The wilderness soon made obsolete and alien the old ideas of rank, caste, and inherited aristocracy," writes conservationist Peggy Wayburn. "Common man could be uncommon man." It was the great sprawl of wild nature that launched a raft of fantasies about our being a chosen people. Nature that served as a resting place beyond the excesses of industry. Nature that provided the first blush of tradition in a culture suspicious of old ways.

My own particular itch to leave the timothy and the dandelions—to walk 140 miles from my front door in south-central Montana to that most remote spot in the country, to catch the early tide of summer in that area and ride it all the way to fall— was never about paying respects to lost paradise. Make no mistake about it, the Thorofare, like a precious handful of other locations in the West, is extraordinarily wild, a place of bugs and blowdown and bears, a landscape with strange and uncertain siren songs. All but the excessively outfitted will sooner or later sweat or freeze or be blown batty here, will lay out in sleeping bags and listen to branches snapping outside the tent and find themselves nearly too unsettled by thoughts of grizzlies to wander out and dump their bladders. In an age when nature gets offered up mostly in magazines and on television shows—like slices of pie, like a morphine drip—this is a place too sprawling to fit on the page, too unkempt for the calendar on the refrigerator door, too vast even for big screen digital high definition TV.

Yet given the fraying edges of the ecosystem, given a growing number of species unable to sustain themselves outside the wild core of Yellowstone—living in what biologists often refer to as a mortality sink—the time seemed right for a closer look. My intention was not only to get a sense of how some of the creatures in the Thorofare are doing, but also, to gain a glimpse of the future. To gauge what the coming years might hold based in part on the impact such places still have on people's lives. Greater Yellowstone, after all, is arguably the best we can muster, no longer intact merely by default, but design. No region in the country is under more scrutiny than this one, none more thoroughly researched and fought over and speculated about. To the degree America can yet muster stewardship for unfettered places, its commitment will likely never be greater anywhere than what it is here, in this so-called middle of nowhere, between the Tetons and the Beartooths, the Absarokas and the Centennials. To the degree we can preserve the dynamic processes of greater Yellowstone, there will be hope for other places. To the extent those processes fall apart, so will go others, many with hardly a whisper.

And so it happened that, on a warm day in June, my friend LaVoy Tolbert and I walked through the front door of my house and headed two miles up the highway to a trail at the foot of Mount Maurice, gritted our teeth and climbed 4,000 feet onto one of those high, sprawling plateaus of the Beartooths, heading west. Our destination was an old guard station perched above the Yellowstone River called Hawks Rest, just two miles south of that most remote spot in the lower 48. Rustic as a pack rat's nest, beautiful as a quag full of camas lilies. We would be cabin tenders, the Forest Service told us, responsible for fixing up the building, mending fences, meeting the public. We'd keep a journal of the comings and goings of various wildlife for park biologists, mark illegal salting sites for the interagency grizzly team. The kind of job a person dreams of long before he gets there, misses long before he leaves.

THE DAY IS BRILLIANT, the sun pouring down at 10,000 feet with that sharp blue tinge of summer in the high country. After what seemed like endless drought, the May snows were back again this year, prompting a grand show of wildflowers, the seeds of many having lain dormant for years. Every footstep falls beside alpine forget-me-nots and the pink, elfin blooms of moss campion. There's the lemon of cinquefoil as well as great splatters of blue from penstemon and bluebell. Wet meadows show themselves from miles away, revealed by the unmistakable creams and ivories of globeflower and marsh marigold. And underlying it all is a mat of grasses and forbs as green as Ireland, reaching from the toes of our boots into what for those on foot is quite literally the middle of tomorrow.

This high up the growing season shines for a couple of months and then fizzles like a cheap sparkler. Such brevity with fierce, shredding winds has resulted in a gathering of plants that never manage to grow much beyond ankle height. A land of crouching gardens. Winter snows pile to depths of 20, 30 feet, sometimes at a rate of 6 feet in a single storm. Winds can reach a hundred miles an hour and, on any given day in late December or January, exposed skin will freeze in a matter of seconds. Spring doesn't even think of showing up in these parts until late May and, even then, no sooner does she stick a toe in the room before the door gets slammed on her foot—over and over, until the sheer weight of her finally wears winter away, turns ice to water, snow to rain. And then at last June, when slabs of granite loosened by the freeze-thaw cycle begin falling in great crashes along the upper shoulders of the distant peaks. A kind of starting gun, if you will, signaling the beginning of a race to bloom before ice reappears just ten weeks later.

Grasses and sedges are scattered everywhere, in part because they remain nearly unscathed by the relentless pawing of the winds, while much of the rest of what grows here are cushion plants, matlike vegetation composed of folded, ground-hugging leaves that not only avoid the wind but also trap heat. On any given summer day temperatures inside the leaves of a cushion plant may be 20 degrees warmer than the surrounding air. Those same folds have another benefit too: They catch tiny pieces of leaves and other debris that might blow by, thereby slowly raising the thickness of the underlying soil, maybe an inch or so every thousand years. The vast majority of these plants are perennials. Winter buds are held low, tucked right at or just below the surface of the soil; more than a few are wrapped in dark-colored hairs that trap heat and warm the emerging flowers. Others wear a kind of peach fuzz—a coating that not only limits the amount of moisture lost to evaporation, but also serves as a kind of solar shield, throttling down the ultraviolet in a place that gets 25 percent more light and twice the radiation of sea level.

Trekking across this, the largest contiguous reach of tundra in America, offers hikers a kind of suspended rapture. Dizzy vistas tumble off in every direction. Underfoot are lilting plateaus, their treads and hummocks rising like ocean waves as far as the eye can see. To the west behind Hellroaring Plateau are the distant peaks of the central Beartooths, while in the other direction, some 5,000 feet below, the Clarks Fork of the Yellowstone River flashes in the sun. Fifty miles to the northeast, along the southern reaches of the Crow Indian Reservation, the Pryors bristle with mature stands of Douglas-fir. And then the Crazy and the Snowy ranges, the Bull Mountains, and the Bighorns, the latter surrounded by a long grassy spill of the Great Plains. Crossing such country is a waltz best measured by the hour, by the footstep, by the inch.

This sense of being suspended, of swimming outside the normal passing of hours, is underscored by the slow, patient tick of alpine life. Along the crests of certain high, exposed ridges to the northwest lie clusters of nearly prostrate trees—commonly referred to as krummholz, or elfin timber—some having sprouted roughly around the time Pilgrims stepped off the boat at Provincetown; after 400 years, the trees are no thicker than the business end of a baseball bat. The buttercups growing at our feet manage to produce only a single cell during their entire first year of growth. This lone cell then divides the following growing season, forms a bud in the third, and finally, after four years, unfurls a bright yellow bloom the size of a thumbtack. Even the larval stages of insects, which at lower altitudes last for roughly a month, may extend here for years.

When I first began imagining this long ramble across the tundra, I figured on making the journey alone. Despite the pleasures of companions, after all, even the best of company will keep you at arms length from the loneliness, apprehension, and all the other wrinkled upshots of being neck deep in the wild—struggles that on days both good and bad can pry open all manner of ducky insights. But one afternoon at a conference in West Virginia, in a move that surprised even me, I blurted out an invitation to 68-year-old LaVoy Tolbert, the former education director at one of the nation's best wilderness therapy schools for troubled teens. I'd first met him in that role during the late 1990s, showing up one day on his doorstep to write about the program; let's just say he wasn't happy to see me. The look on his face was in fact something you might see the father of the bride wearing on having spotted the town drunk at his daughter's wedding. Some would call him unreasonable, ornery. But LaVoy Tolbert is a curmudgeon only to those he thinks might compromise those things most important to him, which at the time included the careful, patient mending of those dispirited kids. And I could hardly help but like a guy like that.

If anyone knows about using nature as a tool for drawing out those aforementioned ducky insights, LaVoy knows it. He talks often about how people had long gone to the wilds to figure things out, make adjustments. Beyond the mere challenge of being out in such places, he often says, it was a matter of credentials. "Out in nature you've got 4.6 billion years of success—the best of everything, the finest the world has come up with, all around you, night and day. Go out for a stroll in the woods and you walk among champions." Kind of like the farmer, he once told me, who each week takes his old plow horse to the racetrack to run against the Thoroughbreds. One day a friend stops him, asks why he keeps paying entrance fees to run races he can never win. "You're right about that" says the farmer, rubbing his chin. "That old horse ain't got a chance. But then he sure does like the company."

You might say LaVoy and I are ripe for that kind of company. Our lives are being torn open by new seasons—mine by a crossing into the heart of middle age, his by what he senses as the beginning of physical decline. Not that we don't still turn stupid at the mere thought of the high country, using a day in the mountains as a kind of corkscrew to untap all the piss and vinegar still running in our veins. But these days we're prone to squeezing other things from nature. Older lessons, deeper comforts. All morning I've been reaching back, thinking about how I ended up in such a place to begin with, 1,500 miles from where I spent my turn as a kid—buttoned to a big yellow swipe of northern Indiana, neck deep in the corn and the rust. With the lone exception of the St. Joseph River, which passed five blocks from my house on a sluggish meander from one end of town to the other—thus inspiring the whimsical name of our fair city, South Bend—it was land straight and tight as a bedsheet, the turnpikes and rail lines and county roads laid out true to the cardinal points of a compass. We spent our lives on the level, as some Hoosiers put it, a condition that almost certainly had something to do with one of the great underlying illusions of the Midwest—namely, the persistent notion that whatever else happened in life, we could at least count on staying found.

But staying found was for me never much of a priority. Walking on Sunday mornings with my parents the three blocks to Our Redeemer Lutheran Church on Wall Street—face still red from scrubbing, a fresh slick of Vitalis in my hair—I often wondered why God plunked me down in such a place, on land bereft of even a good hill to scream down on a bike or a skateboard. Poster child for the topographically challenged. No one was much surprised when about age eight I started hanging out with the only vertical I could find—the giant oaks, maples, and sycamores stitched across a slice of River Park—which I climbed at every whipstitch for nothing more than the chance at a decent view. One blistering Saturday afternoon in July I scrambled down from the trees to tell my parents I needed a job of some sort, a way to fund this brilliant plan to take a big cardboard washing-machine box and fasten to it a hundred helium balloons, a buck each at the farmer's market, thereby flying out of our postage-stamp backyard to points unknown. Lying in bed at night, reviewing the mission, in my mind's eye I was forever looking down not on the smoke and steel of Bendix, Uniroyal, and Dodge, but across an imaginary pouf of ragged woodlots and abandoned fields to the north, beyond the Michigan border, across a loose rumple of hills with blue-green lakes puddled in their bellies.

It was about this same time, the season of my pending ascension, when sentenced one morning for one crime or another to an hour of sitting in the big stuffed chair in our living room, bored senseless, leafing through a stack of magazines, I stumbled across an ad for a Montana vacation kit. Two weeks later, a big white envelope came stuffed with maps and postcards and photos of scrubbed families in flannel shirts smiling from atop horses, and in almost every background, lines of snow-covered peaks, scary and thrilling and vertical beyond my wildest dreams. If novelist Lawrence Durrell was right, that we were in fact "children of the landscape," then in my young mind Indiana would've been the pasty mother—scrunched brow, fingers forever squeezing worry from her hands. The Rockies, on the other hand, were beautiful cousin, rich aunt, and lunatic uncle all rolled into one. I was going to move West, I announced, to the Rocky Mountains, and in a new round of manic behavior set about planning an escape to Colorado for the following year—a 3,000-mile round-trip journey, to be made on my metallic purple Sears sting-ray bike. I finally made it nine years later—made it for good—rolling up the Sawtooths in a 1964 Pontiac with the same name as John Muir's dog.

SHORTLY AFTER NOON, LaVoy spots three brown lumps lying on a hillside a good half mile away. Moving cautiously we're able to approach within several hundred yards, where we finally recognize them as three bull elk, bedded down near the head of Spring Creek. On sighting us they rise slowly and begin moving north, where they're soon joined by four cows; the small herd then ambles together toward the lip of the plateau. Convinced the show is over we stand for a time admiring how healthy they look, the brush and color of their coats. Just as we're about to leave, LaVoy tosses a quick glance behind us toward the head of Spring Creek and notices several animals slipping into a small ravine. Raising my binoculars to the darkest member of the group, at first I think bear. No sooner does that thought hit the ground when the black face of the lead animal turns toward me. Something else entirely. Wolves.

There are six adults—two black and four gray—all without collars, moving on what seems a certain collision course with the elk. Sure enough, partway up a small ravine the pack catches scent of the elk herd, at which point every wolf drops into stalking position. This behavior, which I have seen countless times in Yellowstone, is a reminder that, as in most predator-prey relationships, with wolves and elk there are clear rules to the game, nearly all of them meant to conserve energy. It's not at all unusual to see wolves lope by elk with little response; let them drop to hunting posture, though, and the herd tunes up fast. In the lead this afternoon is a large black animal, likely the alpha female, and it's her actions that control the movement of the pack. We watch her lope toward the head of the ravine, easily crossing a steep, rugged boulder field without a stumble. At the same time the other wolves shift left, and when their leader tops the ravine the startled elk double back, leaving them suddenly facing the rest of the pack. The chase is on: Two elk bail off the edge of the plateau at high speed, but the wolves ignore them, choosing instead to work those that remain, singly and in pairs—running them, watching for stumbles, limps, even hard breathing, any of which could be a sign that an animal is catchable.

Not once do any of them break into high speed. The elk run just fast enough to stay ahead of their pursuers, while the wolves run only hard enough to get the information they need to size up the situation. At one point one of the bulls, perhaps bored with the whole sordid affair, turns to face the wolf that's chasing him. And with that the wolf walks away. His fellow pack members give up at precisely the same moment and settle onto the tundra with paws in front of their faces, tongues out, panting. LaVoy's astonished. In part for having had the great fortune to stumble across this spectacle, especially given that this is probably the only wolf pack within 30 miles. But more than that, having for years heard that wolves prey only on the weakest animals and dismissing such claims as wishful thinking, he's seen exactly that. "My whole take on wolves just shattered," he says breathlessly, still trying to get his head around the idea. "This is one of the great experiences of my life." We see the wolves again about a mile later, lying about on the tundra. Being no fans of humans they glance our way, get up, and saunter into a shallow ravine.

In the seven years since wolves were reintroduced into greater Yellowstone, there's never been a resident pack on the northeast side of the Beartooths. The best chance for that slipped away six weeks after the initial release, on a sage-covered hill outside the old mining town of Bearcreek, when a local woodcutter pulled a borrowed rifle out of his truck, leaned against the door, took aim, and blew the alpha male away. Shortly afterward the pups and their mother were carted back to Yellowstone and released in the park the following fall. As of this summer of 2002 there are roughly 250 wolves in two dozen groups scattered around the ecosystem, the majority living where the elk are most concentrated, on the northern ranges of Yellowstone National Park.

Wolves have now met the target populations set forth by the U.S. Fish and Wildlife Service in the reintroduction plan, which encompasses recovery zones in Idaho, Montana, and Wyoming.

All that's left before they can be removed from the endangered species list (other than making it through the inevitable lawsuits) is for each state to craft an appropriate management plan—a clear strategy for how both the animal and its habitat will be managed in order to keep populations from dwindling again in the future. Wyoming is only now stumbling through theirs, having taken time out to first tend to such important matters as making claims against the federal government to reimburse them roughly $4,000 for every elk taken by a wolf—a monetary amount equivalent, they say, to lost hunting revenues. In all it's a move with about as much integrity as a Jerry Springer guest list, especially when you consider that at the same time the state's been trying desperately to reduce elk numbers in the southern Yellowstone herds. Then again, this is the same legislature that seven years ago voted a $500 bounty on wolves, then passed a law requiring the state attorney general to defend anyone prosecuted for killing one.

Idaho and Montana are further along with their management plans, though Idaho did pause long enough in 2001 to dream up RS 11108, "calling for and demanding that wolf recovery efforts in Idaho be discontinued immediately and wolves be removed by whatever means necessary." Still, some of us are naive enough to hope they've left behind the antics surrounding the initial reintroduction during the mid-90s—a kind of golden era of lunacy when Idaho's governor asserted his right to call out the National Guard and state representative Bruce Newcomb stumped for secession from the Union. At roughly the same time, Montana was busy concocting Joint Resolution Number 8, which called for the reintroduction of wolves to "Central Park in New York City, the Presidio in San Francisco, and Washington,

D.C.," as it was only those damned liberal city dwellers who wanted the things in the first place. (Proving yet again, as a writer for *The Atlantic* suggested in 1898, that "the Montana legislature is probably the funniest governmental body in the world.") Never mind that in a national poll conducted in 1996 by Colorado State University 75 percent of Democrats, 76 percent of Republicans, and 82 percent of independent voters were in favor of the reintroduction; closer to home, in the northern Rockies, opinion was split roughly in half. And finally, there came that brilliant attempt at prescience by Montana U.S. Senator Conrad Burns, who told educator Pat Tucker, "Little lady, mark my words, if they put wolves in Yellowstone, there'll be a dead child within a year."

People often ask me if negative attitudes about wolves in the region have changed since the reintroduction. Some of my rancher neighbors confess to being relieved, glad to have been wrong about how bad livestock predation would be. But it's hardly the sort of thing they'd admit in public. In fact, unless you're up for a blistering argument, it pays to think carefully about what comments you happen to toss out about wolves, and where. To this day you'd probably sooner get the crap knocked out of you for walking into the Bullsitter Lounge in Cody with an "I Love Wolves" T-shirt on than by standing on the bar in a bin Laden T-shirt trying to recruit members for al Qaeda.

An hour or so after the second wolf sighting, we stop to catch our breath on the eastern edge of the plateau, pull out our binoculars, and, in seconds, spot nearly two dozen nanny and kid mountain goats dancing down a sheer wall of igneous rock near Line Lake. Barely two days out and already we've stumbled into a wildlife cabaret. Toss in a grizzly and a moose and we'll have a grand slam. Of course, while many such encounters are pure luck, some of our success has to do with LaVoy's method of travel—that of a hunter, walking always slowly enough to look around, pausing often to sit with his elbows propped on his backpack for a careful glassing of the distant hills. The kind of movement I imagine having once been fairly common, but today so rare as to make it something of an oddity.

We continue this blissful ramble through much of the third day—until lunch, anyway, when we gain a lonely ridge in the Beartooths high above Littlerock Canyon. In a nearby bog, miles from any discernable road, is an abandoned 1947 Chevrolet Stylemaster mired up to the axles. Picked clean of usable parts, sandblasted by the wind, and overwhelmed by the terrain, it seems a comforting monument to the limits of machines, a reminder that even General Motors can be stopped by nothing more than a good wet spot in a high meadow. It's right here, a stone's throw from the middle of nowhere and with more than a hundred miles still to go, that the scope of our journey finally begins to sink in. Westward from this windy perch is a daunting vision of the snow-covered Absaroka mountains. Exploding from the Earth on the far side of the Clarks Fork Valley, they are both beautiful and awesome, a range born of ancient seabeds— the eldest some 350 million years old—later covered by volcanic flows, those in turn eroded by mudflows and water and ice. Without question this is one of the most rugged stretches of high country anywhere in the Rockies. We stare out at the peaks through bites of jerky and cashews and cheese, and all the while they manage to both thrill us and break our hearts. From where we sit there's no hint of any sort of reasonable passage. Yellowstone, lying on the far side, seems all but out of reach.

So we procrastinate. Which for us means launching into yet another prolonged *My Dinner with Andre* kind of conversation, talking of things both lunatic and inspired. The kind of exchange trapper Osborne Russell was fond of, often referring to it as the Rocky Mountain College. Over the past few days LaVoy's stories have been spilling out all over the tundra—more tales than Carter's has little liver pills, as he would put it. This is what I know so far. His crippled right arm was damaged at 14 when, on a bet from friends, he roped a cow high on locoweed. The cow charged the horse, and in the ensuing fracas the rope got wrapped around his right arm, nearly severing it, permanently damaging the nerves. He's got a little use of the fingers on that hand, but not much. His parents, utterly devastated by the accident, hauled him to one doctor after another, each one assuring the family that the cure was close at hand, one failed surgery or therapy leading to the next, until finally, two years later, LaVoy himself put a stop to it. Even with the injury he remained remarkably athletic, playing baseball by mastering a tricky maneuver of catching the ball using his good left arm and then instantly removing the glove to throw it with the same hand. (So good was he at this little juggling act that in his final year of high school he was scouted by the pros; the scout liked what he saw, but in the end decided the injured arm didn't allow LaVoy to get enough muscle in his batting.) There was track and wrestling, too, and in college, a boxing stint that led eventually to an invitation to the Golden Gloves.

LaVoy's story is more, though, than just another tale of boy makes lemon out of lemonade. In the wake of the roping wreck, LaVoy saw a lot of so-called friends distance themselves— turn their backs and even snub him—for the most part because the accident left him looking different, and in high school different is an almost unforgivable circumstance. "I'd always stood up for the underdog," he says, explaining how before the accident he'd be the one to throw in with the weaker kids at school, helping them stand up to bullies. "Now all of a sudden it was me. I was the underdog."

We press on toward Littlerock Canyon, picking up our first obvious path since climbing Mount Maurice on the morning of the first day. The trail drops across open slopes dotted with cow elk and their rust-colored calves, turns south, and then finally heads west through slotted canyons filled with the chatter of fast-running creeks. Once off the tundra the heat comes on, wearing us down, until by and the end of the day we're grimy and bedraggled, sweating up a long, steep run of sopping meadows. It's well after seven o'clock when we finally gain a small crest and call it quits on a rock-strewn tableland cupping Top and Dollar Lakes. The woods, as well as the north faces of the rumpled hills, are thick with wedges of snow; thin sheets of meltwater are coursing across the ground, leaving barely enough dry land to pitch a tent. As yet there are few mosquitoes, though that'll no doubt change fast in the days to come as nighttime temperatures creep back above freezing. I'm tired as hell and LaVoy is close to shot. Two months from now he'll look back on this day as the hardest of the whole summer.

Sitting around the stove waiting for the water to boil, tearing at pieces of jerky, LaVoy pulls back the covers on his childhood again, this time focusing on a favorite topic—his animals. He tells of a certain gelding named Dusty his family captured from a herd of wild horses roaming the high desert not far from his home in southern Utah. One day he and his dad and uncles were out riding near the wild herds again when Dusty—traveling without a rider—sighted his old mates, tore loose, and started running, coming alive as if by magic, herding mares as if he still had all his original equipment. LaVoy chokes a little on the memory, tells me it broke his heart to see the way that horse slumped at the end of the day when the bridal went back on, that the mere sight of it caused him to make some firm conclusions about the worth of freedom.

And then there was Spot. The stupidest dog in Millard County. Supposedly a hunting dog, but one that couldn't be trained if his life depended on it—running ahead of the shooters, ignoring commands, bolting at the sound of gun fire to cower under the truck. But 16-year-old LaVoy noticed something about that dog that everyone else missed, namely that here was a critter with an incredible nose. Time and again he watched as Spot picked up the scent of birds hundreds of yards away, then walked right to them. Describing what he says was one of the most important lessons of his life, LaVoy decided that instead of getting in a twist trying to teach the dog to hunt in the conventional way, he'd instead adjust his own behavior to match the dog's talents. Who cared if Spot drifted out ahead, found the birds, and just stood there until the hunters finally caught up. Let him do it his way. In no time LaVoy was fielding calls from his uncles, from all his dad's friends, every one of them asking if they could come hunting with Spot.

Sitting on this rock, stirring a pot of soup, it dawns on me that LaVoy is one of the few men I've met who talks openly about the insights he gained as a kid. Maybe it has something to do with all the time he spends in the wild. The truth is that even the most distant man seems somehow more willing to fly his daydreams when his chest is pinned under some big, lonely expanse, under black skies shot full of stars. While women are able to take what happens on the job, at home, in the garden and weave a religion out of it, guys seem prompted to such inspiration mostly when they're adrift in some grand stewpot of metaphor. Men are epic junkies. Responsive to those times when life is crushed only to rebound right before their eyes—as so often happens out here, one season trampled by rockslides and windstorms and blizzards, the next rising in a wash of leaves, in great clatters of geese dropping from the sky.

LaVoy's life has long been tethered to such metaphor—not just when he was a kid, but across some 40 years as a high school science teacher. I recall first meeting up with him in the field as he was squatting under a juniper beside a group of 15- and 16-year-old girls, students from that wilderness therapy school, ostensibly teaching biology. "Remember those big mushrooms we ran across earlier today?" he was asking them. "We called them puffballs, didn't we? Well, those puffballs are a good example of life reproducing by spores, millions of them, each one exactly alike." I listened as he then slowly, and with great patience, drew out their ideas about what might be the limits of such a reproduction strategy.

"If I'm understanding you right," he finally said, "the only chance a puffball spore has for success is to land in exactly the right environment. The same conditions as the parent plant." Then more discussion, with the girls concluding that most life doesn't clone itself like that at all, but reproduces sexually—a strategy offering nearly limitless potential for variety. And that with variety comes a better chance for a species to flourish in changing circumstances. "So what you're really saying," he summed up, looking each girl in the eye, "is that nature loves diversity." And in the days that followed that session I watched girls who just weeks before were bleeding from the jagged edges of all that had broken in their lives, staring out past the ponderosa onto the magnificent red rock of Capitol Reef, letting out breath, gathering up the pieces.

Summer in the northern latitudes brings the chance to swim in daylight—a good 17 hours of it, more if you count the powdery blush that comes on in the east before dawn, or the shimmer of alpenglow, which these days lasts well past ten o'clock. Despite the hard trek yesterday, we rise shortly before 6 a.m., by 6:30 are packed and moving, choosing always to eat breakfast down the trail a mile or two or three, when the blood is flowing and the kinks are out—when Arthur, as LaVoy calls the arthritis in his feet, has been all but forgotten. Yesterday I told him I was feeling acclimatized, better adjusted to life two miles up, but he looked doubtful. "You never really get acclimatized," he said. "You just get used to the pain."

By most standards we're traveling light, 45 pounds for me and barely 40 for LaVoy. I've spent two months dehydrating food—everything from spaghetti sauce to salsa, from chicken curry to spinach-lentil soup. An hour or so before eating we pour the dried meal into a quart Nalgene bottle, add water, and walk on; with the jostling of the final miles comes dinner, ready to heat and serve. Besides rain gear and Capilene underwear we carry a few first-aid items, including moleskin and Spyroflex for blisters, some jerky and gorp and a water filter, notebooks, a camera, binoculars. Because we typically eat before getting to camp (thus keeping the smell of food well away from us), the routine at the end of the day is easy. Fifteen minutes to set up the tent and pull out headlamps and notebooks for journaling, ten more to brush our teeth and hang the food bag.

Tonight I'm recalling some hiking advice offered by a stalwart, if snippy, little adventurer by the name of Hanford Henderson. In 1898, Henderson became one of the few people to ever walk the entire loop from Mammoth to Lake to Canyon and back, a journey of more than a hundred miles. Traveling by stage the trip took six days; Henderson did it in five. To walk successfully, he wrote, one has to attend to certain details, the most important being one's dress.

> The common mistake is to wear too heavy clothing and too much. Better venture upon the trip, as I did, wearing the lightest underclothing, a summer traveling suit, a straw hat, and light shoes. A special caution is needed against heavy shoes. They have wrecked many a promising expedition. It is much better to go tripping daintily along, picking one's way, if need be, than to wear tiresome clod-hopper shoes, and step on every sharp stone you see. In my hand I carried a light umbrella (to kill rattlesnakes and frighten off bears) and a modest little paper bundle, in my pocket a package of soda crackers, in my heart many things. Nevertheless, it was very light. This is also important.

Curiously, Henderson wasn't the first to employ an umbrella for protection against wildlife. Theodore Roosevelt relates the tale of a man in Yellowstone trying to see how close he could get to a sow bear with cubs, only to have the animal chase him down and issue a severe bite. The fellow's path of escape was directly at his wife, who simply brandished her umbrella and beat the bear away. Likewise, a 19th-century Montana hunting guide by the name of Farrell routinely traveled not with an umbrella, but with a wooden stick, claiming that "a crack on the nose is worth a dozen random rifle shots."

All the next day we spend leaving the Beartooths. It begins with a quiet walk on a jeep road thick with snow, where we spot our first grizzly tracks, followed by an icy ford of the outlet at Chain Lakes, all the while massive cutthroat trout swimming around our legs. The views to the north are extraordinary. This is the very heart of the Beartooths—colossal turrets and parapets of granite rising some 2,000 feet, blanketed in more snow than I've seen in years. Of all Montana's mountains, these are the ones most likely to crank their own weather, producing squalls and blizzards in every month of the year, freaking out summer visitors from Iowa and Kansas and Michigan steering their giant RVs down the Beartooth Highway, tightening fists and twisting faces, creating a brisk trade in brake repair for mechanics in Red Lodge. Whatever poetry there is in these tumbles of rock is on many days less meter and rhyme than feral, howling free verse. Only now and then does Robert Browning's rosy earth show itself, his lovely, bucolic dew-pearled hillsides. More often it's Whitman, Ginsberg, maybe Gary Snyder: "Ice-scratched slabs and bent trees, / ... / Only the weathering land / The wheeling sky, ..."

It's been just over a hundred years since eight men huddled around a campfire northwest of here, outside the village of Cooke City, Montana. Fresh in from the East they'd come with the charge of making the first in-depth geological exploration of these mountains, known at the time as the Granite Range. In the group was a rough and ready Norwegian photographer named Anders Wilse, a couple of engineers, and a few bearded, fly-bitten hunters and horse packers. And the guy in charge of the show, mineralogist James Kimball, a wad of Rockefeller's money in his pocket.

Not that they were the first rock hounds to show up here. Geologist William Holmes had been in these mountains 20 years earlier, part of Ferdinand Hayden's 1871 survey of Yellowstone. But his reports on the Beartooths had mistakes in them, big ones, leaving Kimball thinking that the guy never really visited the heart of the range at all. And then there'd been General Philip Sheridan in 1882, marching east out of Cooke City past Beartooth Butte, down Line Creek Plateau, and on to the Yellowstone River. But Sheridan was simply doing what he did best—making time, dreaming up roads. The way Kimball figured it, the job of exploring the region was still to be done and he and his partners would be the ones to do it. Sitting around the fire, the men's spirits were high. The final weeks of summer lingered before them like a good dream.

What the party didn't count on was Beartooth weather. On they plodded, making one wind-blasted day trip after another into the unknown: to the head of the East Rosebud, to Lake Abundance and the Stillwater and the Sawtooth summit, up much, but not all, of Montana's highest mountain, Granite Peak. Kimball's descriptions are a mix of scientific jargon—talk of porphyritic dykes and feldspathic granite—and boyish thrill at the steep gorges choked with rocks, ice-formed lakes, and water-falls by the dozen. And always the "treacherous weather—pelting hailstorms, bleak winds," including a bivouac at Goose Lake that would leave him for years afterward referring to the place as Camp Misery.

Kimball's party progressed by splitting up observation chores. As often as not the photographer Wilse gathered his heap of heavy equipment and set out alone across the most rugged of the terrain, ripping his boots and clothes to shreds on the sharp rocks, carrying only a wool blanket and a sack of food, sleeping at night by plucking stones out of the tundra for a patch of grass flat enough to lay down on. It was Wilse who stumbled across the ice field full of frozen grasshoppers that a handful of local hunters and miners had told the party about, a rather famous feature eight miles north of here known as Grasshopper Glacier.

The snows of autumn came early that year, in a few days piling into drifts several feet deep. To their great disappointment the team was forced back to the lowlands, even though there were big tracts of the northern range still unmapped. The trek out of the high country was so difficult that Wilse and an engineer named Wood were assigned the job of scouting ahead of the party for a way out, peering through sleet and snow to locate suitable campsites along the way—preferably near marshy areas so the horses could kick down through the layers of snow to find grass. On the evening of the last day, with the view of the brown, dry prairie stretching before them to the east, Wilse and Wood had an argument about the best way to reach Red Lodge; they split up in a huff and began making solo descents.

Wilse and his horse—a tough mustang with the not-so-tough name of Pussy—had a real time of it. In a diary written years later he describes levering rocks from the snow-covered slope and sending them crashing down the mountain, thereby creating a path on which he could slide down on his rear end, while the horse skittered and scrambled as best he could. It was past dark by the time they reached the bottom, covered in sweat. Meanwhile the rest of the party was stuck topside, buttoned down against 60-mile-an-hour winds. A single tent was finally erected, but the lone person who chose to sleep inside spent the whole night trying to keep the canvas from collapsing against the hot stove, which it did anyway. The next day the party missed the Rocky Fork altogether, landing instead in Wyoming's Bighorn Basin.

Amazingly, following a brief rest at Red Lodge, Kimball and a small party, minus Wilse, took on additional forays in and around the Beartooths all through the month of October: over Dead Indian Pass Road, the sides of which were piled with "snubbing" logs—trees that had been cut and tied behind wagons to keep them from careening out of control on the 2,000-foot, mile-and-a-half-long descent; back around the Beartooths to the East Rosebud, where Kimball watched in horror as 80-mile-an-hour winds destroyed his 12-by-16-foot wall tent, tearing the eyelets out of the fabric and sending clothes, bedding, and even the woodstove flying down the canyon. "Everything had soared away," he wrote, "except blankets under the weight of their possessors. Minor articles, usually worn in pairs, never found their mates. No further adventure proved necessary to force the conviction that endurable conditions for camp life had come to an end for the season."

As for me, it's in the Beartooths where I've gathered the lion's share of my best memories. Up at 10,000 feet with a full moon over some nameless rock-bound lake, mountain goats skimming the edges of camp. Storms coming up as if pulled from a hat, sending me running for the lip of the tundra. Windless dawns propped on an elbow in a bed of forget-me-nots, looking across some 50 miles of nearly empty space at the Crazy Mountains burning in the sun.

ON DAY FOUR, WE LEAVE THE BEATEN PATH AGAIN around one o'clock, plotting a long compass line through the forest over Table Mountain to the Chief Joseph Scenic Highway, hoping to come out at a place called Painter Store. My wife, Jane, will be there, planning to toss on a pack and hike with us for 50 miles— into Yellowstone and up the Lamar River, then into Pelican Valley, coming out near Yellowstone Lake at Fishing Bridge. What we hadn't planned on is Beartooth Creek, just west of Table Mountain—a stream turned insane with snowmelt, rocketing wall to wall through a series of dark volcanic slots, a deadly watercourse that no one in their right mind would consider crossing. We've been told there's a bridge downstream, but when we get to the drainage we find the only tolerable walking to be well away from the creek, which leaves us too far back to see anything. Missing the bridge could take us miles out of our way, leaving us snarled on the banks of the Clarks Fork in a canyon that a skilled mountain goat would be hard-pressed to navigate without ropes and pitons. So we stick close to the east bank of the creek. The channel is pinched by a long series of steep, rock-bound hummocks 50 to 100 feet high; in between are short stretches littered with downed timber, leaving us constantly climbing over, under, and around. The heat is blistering and the mosquitoes have popped out of their watery nurseries to feast on us, mustering their greatest resolve in those moments when I happen to be fully compromised, on my knees or, better yet, on my belly, squirming under downed lodgepole.

After more than an hour of this we spot not a bridge, but a colossal logjam. Four enormous trees lie in a tangle, their bark ripped away by floodwaters, the wood polished to an ivory shine. Underneath is a riot of white water, shouting and shaking not just the logs but the very earth around them. Climbing onto the leading edge requires some acrobatics, and at one point LaVoy actually ends up wedged between two large branches, leaving me having to push like hell to get him through. Of course there's a big difference psychologically between balancing yourself on a log across some dinky creek that might soak your feet and chill your pride and doing it over something that will drown you should you tumble to the upstream side or, should you fall downstream, knock you senseless and rip your pack to shreds in a rock-strewn canyon. When we finally make it over I park myself for a few minutes to get my heart out of my throat. Three more miles to Painter Store, which as luck would have it is closed due to a power outage. But Jane is there. And a bench in the shade. And a cooler full of food.

CHAPTER TWO

ROM HERE ALL THE WAY TO HAWKS REST, across nearly a hundred miles of trail, what will drive the surrounding ecology more than anything else are the fires of 1988. The Clover-Mist fire alone burned nearly 400,000 acres along our route, first charging through Yellowstone to the head of Miller Creek, then crossing the divide into the Shoshone National Forest–utterly ignoring forest officials, who'd stated that under no circumstance would they "accept" fires from Yellowstone. On September 8 the flames roared down Papoose and Crandall Creeks all the way to the Clarks Fork of the Yellowstone, advancing 31,000 acres in a single day. Now, almost 14 years later, vast jumbles of downfall surround a loose weave of standing dead spruce and fir and lodgepole. Every upright tree is wholly or partially stripped of bark, leaving either smooth blond trunks or highly mottled ones, sporting patterns much like those worn by leopards or giraffes. The same forest floor that was once mostly a blanket of pine needles is now a carpet of fireweed and lupine, strawberry and geranium. These are the ghost forests of greater Yellowstone. There is in every season but winter an autumnal feel to them, and the sounds they make are autumn songs. Partially toppled trees lean against those still standing, letting loose a medley of groans and rasps and creaks. These in turn are spiced by a concerto of wind blowing through bare branches—low rushes and hums and, strangest of all, soft, high-pitched strains that sound like young girls off in the distance, singing or mumbling or crying.

Having started to fall 10 to 20 months after the burn, today from 60 to 80 percent of the trees have hit the ground. Looking across the drainages it's possible to identify major wind events by the lay of thousands of flattened trees, as straight and orderly as strands of hair run through a comb. Choosing to go cross-country means crossing acre after acre of downed timber, a feat best accomplished not by stepping over but by staying on top of the logs, dancing from one to the next like the old timber jockeys of the Northwest, riding rafts of cut trees down the rivers to the sawmills. A handful of trail crews are roaming the countryside again this summer, frantically trying to stay no more than one or two steps behind the falling logs. While crews in Yellowstone are able to do the job with chain saws, in the wilderness of the Shoshone and Bridger-Teton National Forests the work gets done the old-fashioned way, with axes and crosscut saws.

Some Yellowstone visitors remain disheartened, even angry, by the destruction they see in the wake of these fires—refusing to believe that the event couldn't have been prevented if only the Park Service and Forest Service had acted more swiftly. But in truth it was a remarkable year. Spring rolled in with higher than normal levels of precipitation, giving rise to thick mats of grasses and forbs. There were enormous fuel loads on the forest floor, in large part thanks to our having spent 75 years suppressing natural fires. Then in June the spigot went dry. By the time lightning began stabbing the earth several weeks later, the moisture content in downed logs was about 7 percent—5 percent less than kiln-dried lumber; moisture levels in small twigs were even lower, a dismal 2 percent. A series of dry cold fronts stoked the winds, which on several occasions reached speeds of a hundred miles an hour. Holding this set of conditions up to more than a century of weather records, it's clear there'd never been anything close to a summer like this.

On July 21, by which point fire had consumed more than 17,000 acres in Yellowstone alone, managers decided to begin suppressing all new and existing burns—both those started by humans (which they'd been fighting all along), as well as those caused by lightning. A month later, on a single Saturday—the aptly named "Black Saturday"—more acres burned than in any decade since 1872; by the following afternoon the fires had grown to more than 400,000 acres. It may be true that a quicker response by firefighters might have saved isolated acreages here and there. But wildfire is one of the great elemental forces of the West and in 1988 it was no more subject to human control than a tidal wave or hurricane or earthquake. By the time that brutal season came to an end, 70,000 fires had burned more than four million acres throughout the West and Alaska.

Of course, the romantic ideal of wilderness has long been a lush one, cool and green and all but free of death. In truth, with wildfire comes great benefits: significant declines in disease; major upticks in the quantity and quality of forage; and, because of the checkerboard nature of most burns, a mixed age class of timber that in time leads to a far greater diversity of bird life. While from a distance these burns may seem stark, those who get close will find here an almost dizzy sense of immortality. Beside our every step rises a flush of young trees 4 to 14 feet tall– as often as not, lodgepole pine. More than any other species, the lodgepole is classic proof that fire has long been woven into the fabric of the Rockies. Depending on the frequency of fires in a given area (this is typically a function of altitude, since more fires occur at low elevations than at high), fully half the trees in a given stand of lodgepole will by age 20 begin producing serotinous cones. Covered with a hard, waxy resin that melts around 113 degrees, these cones open and disperse their seeds only in the presence of fire. Serotinous cones can stand direct exposure to flames for about 20 seconds, which is roughly the time it takes for flames to crown out and consume the canopy of a tree.

In studies done 12 months after the 1988 fires, almost a third of all the new plants in burned areas were lodgepole pines. On good soil, soaked with sun and freshened by loads of nutrients leached from the ashes, seeds were sprouting at the extraordinary rate of 300,000 per acre. Tens of thousands more ended up as food for squirrels, mice, and birds. Since most lodgepole seeds tend to disperse within several hundred feet from the parent tree, it's safe to assume that the stock for much of this new timber came almost entirely from that which was lost to the burn in the first place. Therefore, what was lodgepole forest before 1988 will be lodgepole forest again. During the autumn following the fires Wyoming Senator Alan Simpson told the Senate that the park "may well have been destroyed by the very people who were assigned to protect it. The ground is sterilized. It is blackened to the depths of any root system within it." Actually, not only was there an early abundance of transitional plants such as fireweed, current, and raspberry, but the vast majority of greater Yellowstone was soon rebuilding the same mix of communities present before the burn.

For botanists, hydrologists, and ecologists the fires of 1988 have been the Mardi Gras of natural events, full of surprises— the equivalent of a wildlife biologist getting the chance to unravel the puzzles posed by a major predator like the wolf returning to the ecosystem. It was startling to watch stream communities devastated by the burns recover quickly, only to unravel again under the weight of a large snowmelt the following spring. Likewise, though the sediment load nearly tripled in streams near the headwaters of the Lamar, its effects downstream were much less than expected, perhaps in part because the murky water was being diluted by clear runoff in unburned woods. Barely four years after the fire, sediment in the Lamar River was less than what would have been expected had the fires never occurred. Predictions of massive fish kills—from sediment as well as from a warming of the water due to the loss of tree canopies—never materialized. (That said, trout did perish in some of the more narrow, severely burned drainages—likely the result of intense smoke causing high levels of ammonia in the water.)

Other than in the most extreme conditions, throughout the fire zones elk and deer seemed to move easily, almost casually, around the edges of the flames; meanwhile, at the sound of hovering helicopters, the same animals tensed and ran. One curious black bear was even seen sticking his paw around the flames of a burning log. Though only a small number of species have yet been studied relative to the big burn, so far only two—snails and moose—are known to have suffered significant losses in population. Outfitters, especially, are fond of blaming wolves for a plummet in the moose population; in truth, these animals typically suffer after big fires, as such events often destroy the mature spruce forest that forms an essential component of their winter range.

Burns offer greatly improved vision, which allows us at least the illusion of being better able to deal with the one other major change that comes with having gained the Absarokas. This is full-blown grizzly country. LaVoy, Jane, and I stick closer together, our eyes scouring the land for movement, for certain shapes and colors, often catching our breath before realizing that what we're seeing are stumps crouching in the burn. Reason would tell us not to be overly concerned. Out of 994 grizzly-human conflicts in greater Yellowstone between 1992 and 2000, by far the greatest share involved bears eating human food, killing or injuring livestock, or raiding orchards and gardens. Only 3 percent resulted in injury to people. In fact, since the 1970s, human injuries in the backcountry from bears have averaged roughly one per year. But, of course, all this means nothing when you're lying in your bag at night listening to rustling outside the tent. It's then you tend to think of the 34 deaths and injuries or, if you're particularly masochistic, of the fact that bears aren't inclined to put victims out of their misery quickly, choosing instead to eat first the rich organ meats of their prey. One evening, in a particularly fine show of chutzpah, on hearing a noise outside the tent I'll leap out in my underwear like some sort of unhinged ninja, pepper spray in hand, only to come face to butt with a terrifying mule deer.

We continue to be utterly, splendidly alone. The trail climbs steadily above Crandall Creek, drawing the curtain back on a breathtakingly rugged set of canyons, cliffs, and, far to the west, long green ribbons of tundra. Shortly after crossing Papoose Creek the path braids and dwindles, and moving up the canyon we miss the route at the second stream crossing—a fact duly noted by LaVoy from the sudden absence of horse tracks. We carry on, though, unconcerned, moving west instead on elk trails, our eyes on Bootjack Gap and the eastern edge of Yellowstone, some three miles away. But these paths, too, continue to deteriorate; in several places they're completely washed away by recent floods, leaving only a high, steep bank capped by a line of short, rugged cliffs. LaVoy and I stay lower down, scrambling over loose volcanic soil, at one point moving forward like a couple of over-the-hill Tarzans, swinging on the branches of the occasional lodgepole pine. Jane, on the other hand, seeks a route higher up the slope. Halfway through she suddenly finds herself trapped on precarious footing, stuck fast high above the creek, her only anchor a one-inch ledge of buried rock. Hamstrung, unable to move in either direction, she finally decides to free herself of her pack, letting it slide down the slope into a downed log, where I scramble to retrieve it.

No sooner do I reach it when, out of the corner of my eye, I catch sight of her falling with astonishing speed, heading for the same log that caught her pack, which is spiked along its entire length with stout, broken branches. After a 40-foot slide she comes to rest tucked under the fallen tree—cuts on her hands and arms, a bruise on her thigh, but by no small miracle, nothing more. Even so, all of us are shaken, knowing full well that the plunge could've easily resulted in a serious, even fatal puncture wound. LaVoy and I shake our heads, quietly calculating how long it would've taken for one of us to trek 15 miles out to a phone to secure a rescue. Jane, meanwhile, stands by the creek alone, running the event over and over in her mind, hard on herself for not having either waded the creek or gone higher, onto the more solid footing of the upper cliffs.

It proves only the first of several trials brought on by our decision to stay on the north side of the creek, forgoing the official path for those pounded by elk. Given that these animals rarely travel in stream bottoms, thus avoiding possible ambush by predators, the path stays several hundred feet above Papoose Creek on a fearfully steep side hill, hugging a series of narrow ravines. In places the paths are entirely washed out, leaving for purchase only tiny, broken ledges a few inches wide. Jane's strategy is to go slow, while LaVoy and I scamper across thinking light thoughts, trying to move fast enough so that if one foot slips off we'll be able to recover with the following step. Most of the chutes contain sizable snowmelt streams; crossing them means a delicate dance of leaps and hurdles and hops. After every such crossing the trail vaults steeply upward, levels out, then rounds the next headland only to repeat the same pattern. Over and over. More than a dozen times in all.

And so it is that we come at last to Bootjack Gap, and Yellowstone. Exhausted, hungry, tired, humbled. Over dinner, the sour taste of her nearly disastrous slide all but washed away, Jane turns philosophical. "I figured out why it's so important for me to be out here again," she says, referring to this being the first summer in seven years she hasn't been in the wilds, leading courses for Outward Bound. "I need to feel vulnerable." Life, she confesses, has become safe, and the days she's lived best have always been those at the edge of her comfort zone. It wasn't that the slide was a good thing; clearly, it might well have resulted in tragedy. But it forced her across a threshold of sorts, left her with a presence of mind unknown in more common hours.

Three days later, hiking up the Lamar River, trailing behind LaVoy, I happen to look across the river and see what looks like a shrub some 140 yards away. Suddenly it moves, revealing a fur-covered butt. "Stop!" I whisper, and all eyes turn to a magnificent 600-pound grizzly, huddled over a gravel bar busy with some unknown project. His eyes are squint, his muzzle gray, and thanks to a favorable wind we're able to stand and watch and even photograph for several minutes. No sooner does the breeze quiet, though, when he registers a look of alarm. Shifting his weight to his front feet, straining forward with great determination to place his nose higher in the air, he suddenly catches our scent and is off like a shot.

While it's just the reaction we're hoping for, it's nonetheless curious why such a powerful animal would choose to run at all. Much, if not most of the reason, is no doubt the fact that, since at least the days of Lewis and Clark, humans have consistently removed aggressive bears from the population. In 1898 biologist George Shiras wrote that "the day has gone when any bear in any part of the United States will wantonly attack a man when it is unmolested." Fifteen years later, the great naturalist George Bird Grinnell expressed disappointment at seeing grizzlies rushing away from his hunting party. Still, he explained, such behavior agreed perfectly with accounts he'd gathered from trappers and hunters. "A grisly bear will, in most cases, run away from a man on getting his wind, unless previously wounded, or under such circumstances as to make him think that he cannot escape." This removal of aggressive animals continued in Yellowstone through the 1960s and '70s, when those bears with a habit of causing problems were either relocated, taken to zoos, or killed. LaVoy has another thought on the subject. "Maybe that bear's like some of us," he says of the big bruin on the Lamar. "Just trying to protect his personal space."

The fords of both the Lamar River and Mist Creek are deep and swift, so we cross together, arms to shoulders in a tripod formation. It works well enough, though by the time I reach the far banks the icy water has turned my legs and feet completely numb. From there the trail climbs to upper Mist Creek through lush meadows, their green folds dotted with bison, a half dozen of them grazing under a brilliant sky. And finally, we drop over Mist Creek Pass into the Pelican Valley, landing there early in the morning on the Fourth of July. To the south is the mouth of Astringent Creek, so-named for the high concentrations of alum in the water, full of shrink and pucker. So much so, in fact, that according to 19th-century lore all the animals living along its banks were miniaturized—gaggles of poodle-size deer, beavers no bigger than tea cups.

It was along Astringent Creek that on a snowy March day in 1894 a small detachment of U.S. Calvary was making its way by snowshoe toward the Pelican Valley, tracking a notorious poacher from Cooke City named Ed Howell. Though greater Yellowstone had always been long on poachers, Howell was more infamous than most—a blustery, belligerent son of a gun who'd just as soon shoot you as take a chance on any trouble you might bring him down the road. Howell and a partner had left Cooke City that spring pulling a sledge, heading for lower Pelican Creek where they planned to kill wintering buffalo, dress out the heads, and take them out by pack horse after snowmelt, selling them for $200, even $300 apiece. True to form, Howell had a major squabble with his partner and had run him off, by all accounts with the business end of a gun.

By the time the Calvary caught up to him, Howell had already cached a half dozen scalps in various trees, and was happily going about shooting several more animals in the valley below Astringent Creek, unaware he was being watched from above. If Howell's luck was running low, the Calvary's was running high: The wind was blowing hard, making enough noise to allow the troops, armed only with pistols, to cross 200 yards of open country and make the pinch. At first Howell was calm, coldly informing the soldiers that they'd all be dead had he seen them first. Then, in a move befitting a true villain, he turned on his dog in a rage, attempted to kill the animal for having dropped the ball on guard duty. On their way to deliver Howell to the hoosegow in Mammoth, the Calvary happened across a party of conservationists exploring the park for the enormously popular New York weekly outdoor journal, *Forest and Stream*. One of the magazine's writers, Emerson Hough, dashed off an account of the heroic capture of the nefarious Howell and had the soldiers take it to Fort Yellowstone, where it was wired to editor George Bird Grinnell.

Americans had grown increasingly frustrated with greedy pillagers, from timber barons to ruthless commercial hunters, who routinely raided the public larders of the West. Poaching had been a scourge in Yellowstone from the very beginning; in the spring of 1875 alone, Park Superintendent Philetus Norris estimated that "over 2,000 hides of the huge Rocky Mountain elk ... were taken out of the park." George Bird Grinnell was not only a brilliant spokesman against such waste (he was particularly incensed that in the end Howell's only punishment was to be expelled from the park), but also well connected to those who could do something about it. "So long as these lewd fellows of the baser sort ... know that they will not be punished for their invasions of the Park," he later wrote, "ten regiments of troops could not protect it against their raids." Enlisting the help of the Boone and Crockett Club, Grinnell began an intense lobbying effort for expanded protection of Yellowstone's game animals. In the end Congress said yes to what many consider one of the most significant pieces of wildlife conservation law in American history. It was called the Lacey Act, introduced on March 26 by Iowa Republican and conservationist Congressman John Fletcher Lacey—remarkably, only 13 days after Ed Howell had been pinched by the Army here in Pelican Valley.

We're coming fast to the front country now, and that alone has me on edge. To come out of the wilds after nearly a hundred miles, where but for the lower Pelican Valley we've seen just two parties totaling six people, into the crazy bedlam of curio shops and snarled traffic, is like a man taking breakfast in Provence and then dinner at Wal-Mart. Then again, even circuses have something to recommend them. We stumble out of the wild in midafternoon on July 4. A good friend, writer John Clayton has driven my van to the Pelican Trailhead, loading it first with fat sandwiches, gossip from home, and two gallon-size bottles of Red Lodge Ale. The four of us roll up the highway like so many bohemians, the van piled high not just with people, but with our entire store of food and equipment for the summer, which Jane and John will drive down to a Wyoming outfitter who will then bring it to Hawks Rest by mule string. The staff at the laundry, store, and showers are incredibly solicitous, but, of course, it's still early in the season. Either that or they've opted for some sort of surgery to supersize whatever organ is responsible for allowing a person to be asked 300 times in a week where the bathroom is without going nuts.

At the campground kids shuffle and dodge and ride their bikes around the loop roads at high speeds, kick soccer balls and throw Frisbees and eat ice cream, try to figure out how their older siblings managed to ditch them. Meanwhile their parents are strolling hand in hand, smiling, many speaking German or French or Japanese. A guy about 20 is in the bathroom furiously power washing his mouth with an electric toothbrush, while just outside the door a young woman is parked on a bench, reading Molly Ivins. With darkness comes the twinkling of night lights from a hundred campers, and in the air the smell of burning wood. Big men sit in sling chairs feeding big fires. They seem remarkably content—glad, maybe, to be so fully in control of their world, even if it is just a patch in the woods 30 by 40 feet. By ten o'clock the village has nodded off to sleep.

Following breakfast we head to the Ninemile Trailhead on the east side of Yellowstone Lake, where we find park rangers Bob Jackson and Frank Deluka packing their horses for the season's first trip into the Thorofare. Bob gives us the skinny on fording streams—go upstream at Mountain Creek, downstream at Thorofare Creek, count on them running high but clear. Says he's heard the mosquitoes are especially bad this year. With that he climbs into the saddle and with a wave of his hand is off, about to begin his 26th season in the most isolated outpost in Yellowstone, a stone's throw from the most remote spot in the continental United States.

CHAPTER THREE

*

$\mathcal{B}$ UT FOR A QUIET APRON OF FOREST, A FEW
meadows scattered about, the world south of the
Ninemile Trailhead turns on stunning views of Yellowstone
Lake. At 136 square miles, with 110 miles of shoreline, the
weight of its presence is overwhelming. No piece of Yellowstone
is more likely to change its mood at the snap of a finger, going
from a temper appropriate to Sigurd Olson floating about in his
birchbark canoe to a hair-raising, life-threatening cauldron—
waves running five and six feet high, driven by the prevailing
southwesterly winds. Canoeists in the middle of the lake are
always at risk, and even those who float about in powerboats have
to be prepared to make a dash for shore. The water here aver-
ages only about 45 degrees, which means that the survival time
for swimmers is about 20 minutes. As Yellowstone historian Lee
Whittlesey points out, "No body of water in Yellowstone Park
and probably in all of the United States is more potentially dangerous." Seventy-five years before Gordon Lightfoot sang of

Lake Superior never giving up her dead, the same comment was being made about Yellowstone Lake. Nearly half of all drowning victims here have never been recovered; as for the rest, some have come back in pieces. Roughly a year after an accident in 1906, for example, on two separate days parts of two different men washed up on Stevenson Island—an arm, a leg, a skull.

The area feels progressively wilder as LaVoy and I move south, no doubt in part because we're falling away from the front country. On the afternoon of the second day a pair of large powerboats pass close to shore, each holding scrubbed-looking couples with cocktails in hand. Their attention is elsewhere, though, and they never notice us walking on the high bluffs above the shore. But for them, we see no one. Nearly every feeder stream we cross is flashing with cutthroat trout, part of a million or so returning from the lake to the waters they were hatched in to spawn the next generation. Some will travel only a short distance, while others are making for waters some 20 miles south of the lake, past the door of the Hawks Rest cabin, in the process attracting fishermen from around the country. Grizzlies are gathering on the east side of the lake, as well, doing a bit of fishing of their own. The bad news is that trout numbers have been dropping steadily—whether from drought or the introduced lake trout feeding on them, from whirling disease or reduced spawning success following the burn, or from all of the above, no one can say for sure.

The Yellowstone River approaches the delta like a wanderer not quite ready for home. Twisting and turning, putting on two miles sideways for every one forward, nudging a thousand sweeps of willow, flooding countless side channels full of goldeneyes, teals, and Canada geese. At the very mouth of the river, near the Molly Islands, rows of white pelicans perch on drift logs washed down from the mountains. It will be pelicans that lead us southward to Hawks Rest, spiraling just ahead in great circles, hanging on enormous black-tipped wings above the backwaters and bayous, startling in their ability to seem both heavy and full of grace—size 16 ballerinas, on a planet with half the gravity of Earth. Unlike brown pelicans, which feed by diving for fish, these birds work as a team, surrounding fish and driving them into shallow water and finally scooping them up with their bills. For all their size they are cautious birds, quick to flush from their nests at the approach of intruders, which in turn can lead to the death of their young from exposure.

When native trout populations fell off dramatically around 1915, there were a number of suspects; at the top of the list were white pelicans (this despite the fact that the U.S. Bureau of Fisheries was snapping up millions of "black spotted trout" eggs from Yellowstone Lake each year to plant in waters throughout the West). Henry Baldwin Ward, head of the zoology department at the University of Illinois, compared the pelican directly to the wolf, suggesting their numbers should be strictly controlled by destroying eggs on the primary nesting grounds, right here on the Molly Islands. Meanwhile the Bureau of Fisheries—relying on yet another image used frequently to describe wolves—referred to pelicans as enemies of Yellowstone's fish, otters, and minks, "killers who frequently destroyed far in excess of their needs." Like most conservation decisions in the early 20th century, pelican policies were driven by economics, the value of the bird understood almost entirely in terms of what harm it did to species considered important to sportsmen. Acting on Henry Baldwin Ward's advice, the Park Service began controlling the pelicans of the Molly Islands in 1926, killing some 200 eggs that year, 83 young birds the following year, and, in 1928, every young pelican on the islands.

In that same era white pelican populations were faltering throughout western North America. At Oregon's Upper Klamath Lake, for example, breeding pairs had dropped from roughly 5,000 in the late 1800s to zero in 1931. As the century unfolded, conservationists around the country became increasingly alarmed about the plight of these birds, none more so than a group of disaffected Audubon Society members who had gone off on their own to form the Emergency Conservation Committee. In the lead slot of the ECC was a small, incredibly feisty woman from New York City named Rosalie Edge. During her tenure as chairwoman Rosalie put out dozens of passionate calls to action, including a small brochure called "Last of the White Pelican" in 1931, and the following year, "Slaughter of the White Pelican." (Edge would also prove an eager player in the battle to stop excessive hunting of Yellowstone's southern elk herds, many of which summered in the Thorofare. In 1933 she wrote that the animals were faced with "one of the most cruel disasters in the history of the park ... an orgy of butchery.") The ECC was joined by far more conservative voices, including scientists from the Bureau of Biological Survey and various universities around the country. Finally, in 1932 Yellowstone Superintendent Roger Toll not only issued protection for the pelican colonies—prohibiting any further boat landings on the Molly Islands—but gave a new lease on life to other predators in the park, as well. To no small degree this began a new chapter in American conservation, calling for native animals in the national parks to be afforded protection whether or not they had any obvious economic value.

We're on the home stretch now. The morning of our tenth day finds us at the southernmost point of a classic journey made in 1871 by Nathaniel Langford and Gustavus Doane, a trip that would help set in motion the final push to create Yellowstone National Park. "We had seen the greatest wonders on the continent," Langford wrote after returning to the north end of the lake, "and were convinced that there was not on the globe another region where, within the same limits, nature had crowded so much of grandeur and majesty, with so much novelty and wonder." In the area near the delta the two men had decided it was time for a look around, so they gained a high ridge to the southeast some thousand feet off the valley floor. "The scene was in full majesty," wrote Langford. "The valley at the base of this range was dotted with small lakes and cloven centrally by the river, which, in the far distance, we could see emerging from a canon [*sic*] of immense dimensions." It's at the head of that canyon, where the river turns east and begins reaching for the high flanks of the Absarokas, that LaVoy and I will come at last to the Hawks Rest cabin. Our route will be through a sprawl of river valley almost 25 miles long, the land canted in the sort of modest tilt that makes rivers go from shouts to whispers. The Thorofare. So-called by early trappers for the easy north-south passage it afforded, in a region otherwise blocked by the wide, rugged shoulders of a riotous high country.

OUR TINY TWO-ROOM CABIN, named after a nearby mountain, sits a mile or so from the confluence of the Yellowstone River and Atlantic Creek, perched some 50 feet above the upper meadows in a loose toss of lodgepole pines. Simple from the day it was built, the cabin has been humbled further by the harsh climate, which has scoured the logs and cedar roof shakes to the ashen gray of fallen timber. The logs have been chinked inside and out not with mud or cement, but with a jigsaw puzzle of wood strips, each carefully angled, fitted, and nailed into the clefts formed by adjacent logs. A tiny porch squats beside the front door, barely big enough to set up a folding chair—a kind of box seat for watching the evening sun making for Two Ocean Plateau.

Inside the door is the main living area, not quite 18 feet square. A square, burly table covered in yellow oilcloth sits at the center of the room, surrounded by five small wooden benches. Within arms reach is a pair of stacked bunk beds tucked into the northwest corner, and beside those a wood-burning cookstove and oven. Under the window on the east side of the room is a counter and two-basin sink, fed by a small spring located high on the hill behind the cabin, squatting in the woods in a patch of raspberry. The room's not without its finer touches. Kitchen towels can be draped across an elk antler nailed to the wall above the sink, while another set of antlers next to the beds holds the hats, shirts, and pants of the sleeping. A row of iron skillets hangs on the log wall next to the cookstove; thus a person crawling out of bed in the morning need take only a single step from the mattress to light the woodstove, where he can also pluck a skillet off the wall to begin warming it for pancakes. A stack of large metal tubs in the corner by the sink serve as dishpans and washing tubs, though when it comes to taking baths, a plunge in the Yellowstone River works just as well. Laundry is done outside in five-gallon buckets, a toilet plunger serving as an agitator. Once rinsed the clothes are laid out to dry on the top rail of a wooden fence. They're deemed officially done at the point the wind blows them off the fence.

Cut into the south wall of the main quarters is a door leading to the tack room, which contains another set of bunks, as well as saddle racks, horse feed bins, a small tool bench, and miscellaneous supplies—white gas to lantern parts, horse panniers to bridles, shovels to crosscut saws. Another door leads from the tack room outside to a set of hitching rails. Beyond these, a dirt path winds along the edge of the forest to a log outhouse, the interior of which is heavily scratched with the names of people who've lived or worked here in years past. There are a good dozen carvings by locally famous horse whisperer Jack Hatch, the man in charge of breaking wild mustangs for use by Forest Service trail crews. Other longtimers marking their presence include ranger Gordon Reese and his kids, one of whom was baptized below the cabin in the Yellowstone River. Not to mention countless trail crew workers, having each summer led strings of mules through the wilderness, building bridges and water bars and knocking apart fallen logs with crosscut saws.

A tree branch nailed to the inside wall of the outhouse holds the toilet paper, while a spare roll sits under an inverted Maxwell House coffee can, this to keep the mice from making confetti out of it. The final touch, and a critical one, is a piece of foam padding duct-taped to the top of the plastic toilet seat, offering users both warmth and comfort. For those who by choice or necessity must linger in their duties, the door of the outhouse opens wide to reveal a small view of the Yellowstone River, barely visible some 300 yards away, flashing between scattered branches of Englemann spruce and lodgepole pine.

Of course, while all this is utterly romantic in July or August, it's less so toward the end of hunting season, when answering the call can mean running through the woods at zero degrees only to find the door of the outhouse blocked by drifts of snow. And there can be other hazards as well. Several years ago, while sweating out the inglorious job of digging a new outhouse hole, forest ranger Michelle Tibbetts had the misfortune to puncture her can of bear spray on a rock at the bottom of the pit. Writing in the cabin logbook, she offers a piece of advice parents everywhere would do well to drive home to their children: "Never dig an outhouse hole with your bear spray on your hip."

I describe our little abode with great fondness, but in truth the attraction has come on slowly, choked at first by the condition of the place when we first arrived. Except for an occasional overnight use by trail crews, it'd been years since anyone was stationed here—anyone, that is, other than pack rats, field mice, and an errant marten, who in a psychotic rage knocked over boxes and cans and shredded insulation into piles of flotsam. Mice had long been partying at night in the main living quarters, leaving droppings scattered all over the countertops. A certain pack rat was on a rave of his own, taking care of rat business back in the tack room—the same varmint, we have reason to believe, that, according to a logbook entry on September 27, 2001, chewed a massive hole in a trail worker's brand new Stetson.

Every bit as appealing as this festival of rodents was the grease and crusted bits of food clinging to nearly every dish, pot, pan, and piece of silverware—even on the insides of the cabinets. The catch basin at the spring on the hill had fallen into disrepair and had to be dug out and rebuilt, as did the septic field in front of the cabin. A piece of God-knows-what was lodged in the drainpipe for the sink, which we finally blasted out in a Herculean wrestling match with the toilet plunger. (A couple of friends—one a wildlife vet, the other a poet—happened to be on hand when this feverish overhaul was going on and, in a fit of supreme compassion, they rolled up their sleeves and lent a hand. An act of kindheartedness that no doubt earned them a box seat in the afterlife.) The final icing on the cake was a whining, unrelenting cloud of mosquitoes. Hundreds of them. Inside the cabin. Just as we were about to set up the backpacking tent as sleeping quarters LaVoy discovered an old, crusted sheet of mosquito netting; this he tossed into the five-gallon-bucket washing machine to scour the scum away, at which point we cut it in half and draped the pieces over the head of each bunk. We'll be cowering under that netting every night for the next six weeks.

The Hawks Rest Patrol Station, as well as the Thorofare Ranger Station, located just to the north across the Yellowstone border, was originally part of a string of shelters known as snowshoe cabins. Constructed throughout the backcountry in the late 19th and early 20th centuries, mostly in Yellowstone Park, the snowshoe cabins were meant to offer basic accommodations to winter patrols traveling about by ski trying to nab poachers. Poachers had long before learned that the Army presence was almost nonexistent in the winter, leading many to cache supplies throughout the backcountry so they could operate in relative peace as soon as the snow started falling. The cabins changed all that. The first six were authorized for Yellowstone in 1890, at a cost not to exceed a hundred dollars each. The original Hawks Rest cabin, constructed in 1917, was torn apart in the late 1940s by a strong-willed grizzly; shortly afterward it was dismantled, burned, and the current cabin erected in its place.

As the days go by we add our own touches to the place, anchoring our own routines. A hundred yards from the cabin is a fine old stump I can wrap my knees around and use for a writing table, though in truth the enticing views it affords of the Yellowstone and surrounding meadows are keen distractions. There are hundreds of yards of broken fence to rebuild, broken floors to cobble together, and books to read at night under the hiss and sputter of the white gas lantern: *Lewis and Clark Among the Grizzlies, The Great Gates, The Rocky Mountains, The Great Divide,* not to mention pages and pages of field guides covering birds to bears, shrubs to mushrooms.

Beautiful as it may be, this most remote region in the lower 48 is by far the busiest slice of backcountry either of us have ever seen. Most days it feels as though we've stumbled onto a colossal family reunion—short on kids, long on lunatic relatives. There's that crazy cousin up Thorofare Creek—let's call him Ned—a full-time outfitter and part-time poacher who once shot a mountain lion inside Yellowstone Park and then hung a sign at his camp for all to see (including Bob Jackson, who was tracking him) declaring "[Ned] Gets Pussy." Closer to home is good ol' Uncle John Henry, who every day at twilight turns out 35 head of stock with almost every last animal wearing a bell you could hang in a church steeple, forcing neighboring campers to either stuff their ears with plugs or, more likely, pick up their tents and move away. Also here this week is brother Doug Miller, star of a weekly outdoor show in Salt Lake City—surrounded by coolers and float boats and an entourage of wranglers and production men, smiling into the camera right on cue and assuring tens of thousands back in the land of Deseret that he's found paradise. Meanwhile, many of his fellow campers, including a quiet, thoughtful man from Utah named Mark, stand by and wince. "God," Mark whispers. "I wish he wouldn't do that." Until late August not a single week will pass when Hawks Rest isn't wrapped in shouts and whistles and dog barks and horse bells and beer-soaked snorts and cackles. A nearly endless line of pack strings has been moving past our little cabin; over the next month and a half more than 600 people will pass, along with two or three times that many horses and mules.

Not that such commotion is anything new. Twenty-five years ago, Forest Service ranger Gordon Reese was contacting on average a hundred people every week and spotting close to 400 horses and mules. "Almost without exception," he writes in the logbook in July 1979, "everyone I talked to this summer brings up that there sure are a lot of people around." Reese goes on to say that the sheer volume of visitors is detracting from the wilderness experience. Similar comments show up during the hunting season of the following year, though this time the ranger—one R. Naylor—can't resist capping his official entry with an unofficial rant. "I don't know if it's this crazy during the summer with illegal spike camps, chain saws, horses next to the lake, garbage, fires, rescues, and outfitters crying about everything and us up here without any authority. What they need up here is a platoon of Marines and a few heads knocked together. It sure makes the job exciting, though."

Long before the days of Gordon Reese and R. Naylor, Hawks Rest had a reputation as a magnet for those in search of a little warmth and humanity. In the mid-1930s the cabin was referred to as "convention hall" for the strings of packers and dudes stopping by day and night—more than a few, by the way, coming to listen to ranger Jack Tevebaugh's radio, an especially big hit during hunting season when the world series was on. The guest list was long and varied, rich to poor, including Max Wilde, the Sinclairs, Tex Darling, and banking tycoon Roland Harriman.

That the Thorofare remained so incredibly popular, especially with the saddle crowd, has a lot to do with an onslaught of horse and hunting magazines that promoted it over the decades without mercy, making much of the fact that this is one of the last places in the northern Rockies where stock can be turned out on free pasture. At the same time, the area has long been presented as a Valhalla for the hook and bullet crowd, even though the fishing has grown increasingly marginal as spawning cutthroat populations continue to decline. By the early 1960s Hawks Rest had become a cowboy version of Burning Man. Don Hooper, now in his 70s and living in Kimberly, Idaho, first walked onto the scene as district ranger in the fall of 1961, three years before the passage of the Wilderness Act. He recalls the scene with a pained look. There was a nearly unbroken line of camps, he explains, both along the Yellowstone River and Thorofare Creek—60 or 70 outfitter camps alone—everyone crowded so closely together that their horses and mules were intermingling in the meadows. Hoop, as his friends still call him, tried his best to make regular contact with some of the larger groups, taking the chance to explain ways they might minimize their impacts. "I remember one trip with my wife, when we ran into a single private group of 80 people, with 150 pack animals. You can imagine what happens to a camp under that kind of use."

It was under Hoop's watch that an effort was launched to lessen the crowding by retiring expired outfitter permits. Then, in a desperate attempt to untie the knot of people at Hawks Rest,

Hoop assigned trail crews to start rebuilding old routes in other parts of the wilderness, including Woodard Canyon and along the Buffalo Fork and the upper Yellowstone. Around the time work on the Buffalo Fork was completed there occurred an incident with a large youth camp that proved a precursor of a theme still common today—the wrangling by the powerful for special privileges. The lead packer of the camp was a dyed-in-the-wool cowboy named Jack Davis, who insisted on trailing his mules without so-called pigging strings, which are lengths of line connecting horses or mules to each other, light enough to break should an animal slip off the trail. Without those lines, Hoop explains, his new trails were getting hammered, 50 and 60 mules fanning out all over the place, cutting and eroding switchbacks, deepening bogs.

Hoop discussed the matter with his supervisor, Robert Safran, who agreed it would be a good idea to create guidelines for using the trails, as well as to place some kind of limit on the size of parties. The two men made arrangements to meet with the owners of the camp at the end of the summer season. They got a chilly reception. Still they pressed on with their plan, Safran telling Hoop to write the camp a letter summarizing the new policy. Two weeks later Hoop got an anxious call. "Get down here right away!" Safran told him. "We've got a hell of a problem because of your letter. Boy, are you in trouble."

As it turned out, the owner of the camp happened to be good friends with then-Secretary of Defense Robert McNamara, and on hearing about the policy change McNamara got in touch with Secretary of Agriculture Orville Freeman. "Dear Orv," he wrote. "It seems the Forest Service is sitting kind of hard on my friend regarding his use of the Teton Wilderness. Would you see what you could do to make it easier on him?" From "Dear Orv" the letter went to "Dear Chief" (of the Forest Service), demanding a full-blown accounting of the decision, which in turn went to the regional forester, then finally to Forest Supervisor Safran. Hoop dropped was he was doing and wrote up a detailed explanation of the decision, then sent it back up the line. By no small miracle the plan stood. Even so, Hoop is among several land managers today—though one of the few to admit it publicly—who believes that use is still too high in the Yellowstone meadows, that the resource is being compromised.

There's tremendous appeal to having Bridger Lake, the Yellowstone River, and plenty of pasture within a few hundred yards of your tent; those amenities alone account for much of the heavy use in the Hawks Rest region. Beyond all that, though, a lot of visitors seem no less full of herding instinct than their horses, coming here at least in part to engage in the lost art of neighboring. With a trip to Hawks Rest comes the chance to invite those in adjacent camps over for a Budweiser or a dollop of bourbon, discuss the merits of mustangs versus quarter horses, the beauty of manty packs, how last week a horse foundered in that terrible bog on Atlantic Creek and had to be shot, then later blown apart with dynamite to reduce potential trouble with grizzlies. And speaking of grizzlies, many of the same travelers take no little comfort from the fact that the big bear seems less inclined to attack a small town than a single camp. Given all the guns at Hawks Rest, Army Special Forces would be hard pressed to overwhelm it.

Part of our job this summer is to visit with folks, stroll around and answer questions, make sure no beer or Twinkies have been left out for hungry bears. Yet on any given day there will be plenty of visitors coming to us, as well—men and women saddling their horses and riding anywhere from 300 yards to a mile to the cabin. Some show up in need of help—a horseshoe, maybe, a map or a Band-Aid or even a bed. Others come asking if the fire ban is still on (it always is), while more still want to know if we've seen bears, where the fish are and what they're biting on. All of those together, though, don't add up to the number of people stopping by simply to regale us with stories.

The yarnfest begins only hours after we arrive, when Galen Guthrie comes over on two separate occasions to tell his grizzly story from years ago, which is also faithfully recorded in the cabin logbook. Galen and company, the tale begins, had had a remarkable day of fishing. That evening, and for reasons never fully explained, he and his friends decided to hang their roughly 150 pounds of fish from a tree right in front of the cabin. "Right there," he says, standing on the porch and pointing to a spot barely ten yards away. Galen's entourage included a newlywed couple, who that very night were sleeping in the cabin underneath the window closest to the aforementioned fish hanging tree. When the bride was awakened by an odd sound outside she elbowed her groggy groom, who, still half-asleep, smacked the window to scare the creature off, in the process breaking the pane of glass.

Galen heard the commotion and rushed to the rescue. Assuming he had a black bear on his hands he stormed out into the yard with a flashlight and .22 pistol, testosterone raging, and began yelling—getting very, very close to what in fact did turn out to be a bear. Only too late did he realize it was a grizzly. Which, as you can imagine, dampened his enthusiasm. Anyway, there they were, two predators upright, locked in a fierce standoff, the grizzly moving off to the side by inches, his withering stare locked onto a trembling Galen Guthrie. Of course, Galen wasn't eaten or he wouldn't be here on the porch telling this story for the second time today. Still, not a year passes when he doesn't return to the site of that showdown, relive it with anyone who'll listen, stand there and shudder with them at the thought of what might have been.

CHAPTER FOUR

*T*HE SUMMIT OF HAWKS REST SITS NEARLY
1,800 feet above the valley, looking like the prow of a
mighty ship having sailed west through the stormy terrain of the
Absaroka Range, landing just shy of the banks of the Yellowstone.
There are other, similar-looking formations docked nearby, each
parallel to this one—Yellowstone Point to the south and the three
massive promontories of The Trident to the north. No trails of
any count cross the ridges; cross-country travel tends to be on
a sour mix of loose volcanic soil and cobbly breccia, as well as
over jackstraw piles of trees burned in the 1988 fires, 60 to 70
percent of which now have been toppled by the wind. As a
result, few visitors ever make it to the high lines. Those who do
summit Hawks Rest, though, are rewarded by views into one of
the largest, most extraordinary meadow complexes anywhere in
the Rockies.

To the north lies Thorofare Creek, running through a
gravelly floodplain for nearly 20 miles, tossing back and forth

between its banks with all the swagger of a rumba dancer. Coming to the meadows from the southwest, meanwhile, is beautiful Atlantic Creek, rising from a parent stream that splits in two on the Continental Divide at a place called the Parting of the Waters—one branch going west to the Pacific, the other east to the Atlantic. Finally is a dramatic slice of the Yellowstone, the longest undammed river in America—here calm, dreamlike, having arrived by way of a 20-mile-long tumble from its birthplace among the remnant snowfields of Younts Peak. From this high perch the river appears as a soft blue twist laid across the land like a rope tossed casually to the ground, full of oxbows and meanders, easing past Hawks Rest and then making north for Yellowstone Lake. It's a Western wilderness version of Thomas Cole's famous painting from Mount Holyoke, Massachusetts, "The Oxbow," where the artist dovetails the ideals of the yeoman farmer with another, somewhat contradictory hunger for unsullied nature. Here, though, the farmers have been replaced by outfitters, leading strings of weary dudes day after day through the summer, toting not grain or plows, but collapsible lawn chairs and fly-fishing rods and steaks and beer.

Despite the incredible harshness of the environment, this country has long been occupied by humans. In historic times there were the Sheepeaters, a subgroup of the Shoshone people who moved into the Rockies from the southwest about A.D. 1400. While some early writers derided the Sheepeaters as poor and wretched—in part a judgment based on their lack of horses—others considered them extraordinarily skilled, among the finest hunters and furriers anywhere in the northern Rockies. Nineteenth-century trapper Osborne Russell described them as being "all neatly clothed in dressed deer and sheep skins of the best quality, perfectly contented and happy."

Long before the Shoshone moved into this area there were other travelers, many spending time along the shores of the large glacial lakes to the south, outside present-day Jackson. Trappers and ranchers and finally archaeologists have long written about finding sites littered with projectile points, tools, grinding stones. Even more surprising, though, is the abundance of archaeological records in these highest reaches of the Teton Wilderness. According to the most comprehensive study to date, published in 1998, high elevation areas in the Wind River, Gros Ventre, and Absaroka Ranges yielded on average more than 20 sites per square mile. Current theory paints a picture of the comings and goings that looks something like this:

With the arrival of spring in ancient times people migrated up from the plains onto the shores of the big valley lakes, where they harvested yellow water lilies, balsamroot, wild onion, even spawning cutthroat trout. As summer broke, small family groups climbed thousands of feet into the high country, staying in established camps on the tundra for weeks at a time—not just for the chance at game, which in this area was hunted with projectiles made of local chert, but, just as importantly, for certain high elevation plants: bistort and spring beauty, biscuit-root and whitebark pine. Archaeologists have also found on these high ridges and peaks stone circles measuring some 9 feet in diameter and 18 inches high, generally thought to be vision quest sites. With autumn came a move down to the low country again, more than likely laden with large bundles of dried plants for food and medicine. And so life went for some 8,000 years.

As one looks down from the summit of Hawks Rest, it's obvious that one of the great drivers of life in the Thorofare are the rich meadows—each long twist cut by meandering streams wrapped in willow, and beyond that, open weaves of reed grass, sedges, cinquefoil, and mountain aster. In early summer, moose bluster through the willows while grizzlies sit on their haunches and dig yampa and biscuit-root. Marsh hawks and bald eagles can be seen patrolling the riparian zones, flying over gaggles of Canada geese and Barrow's goldeneyes. Beyond the river are snipes and, farther back still, lark sparrows, their nests tucked out of sight in thick weaves of grass.

For all the creatures here, though, none takes center stage more often in the drama of the Thorofare than do the elk. Ten thousand of them roam the lower reaches of Yellowstone National Park and the northern folds of the Teton Wilderness. They come in groups numbering in the hundreds from the National Elk Refuge outside Jackson, from preserves in the Gros Ventre Range, from sage-covered flats along the Greybull River, navigating enormous drifts to somehow arrive at almost the exact moment snow goes off the meadows. It's the elk that attract the wolves and the grizzlies, the coyotes, and even the occasional mountain lion, as well as scavengers from eagles to foxes, badgers to beetles. And, of course, it's the elk that bring humans, many paying thousands of dollars to outfitters for a once-in-a-lifetime shot at a trophy bull.

When trappers like John Colter and Osborne Russell first wandered through this area early in the 1800s, elk were common high and low, living a somewhat laid-back life by today's standards. Well before the onset of heavy snow, animals in and around southern Yellowstone started a slow meander to winter

range, some drifting west across the Tetons, many more heading all the way to southwest Wyoming, into the Red Desert and
along the windswept banks of the Green River. But as settlements
sprang up, as barbed wire unrolled from an increasingly knot-
ted line of towns and farms and way stations and railroads and
cattle pastures, many of those distant ranges were cut off, leaving the elk to fare as best they could in high mountain valleys
like Jackson Hole.

In a lot of years that wasn't much of a problem. Elk, after
all, can not only feed on a variety of plants in rough country, but
also are much more able than cattle to paw through deep snow.
By the time the first settlers of Jackson showed up on the scene
in the 1880s, wintering elk were already hanging out there by
the thousands, especially around marshy areas north of the
present town site, near the mouth of Flat Creek and Sheep
Creek. But when winters were severe—and in Jackson Hole that
was often the case—the fact that the animals were cut off from
lower country to the south led to mass starvations. In 1890
alone, out of an estimated 50,000 elk wintering in and around
Jackson Hole, some 20,000 are said to have starved. Other large
die-offs occurred in the winters of 1886, '89, '90, and '96, as well
as 1909, when locals were fond of saying that a man could walk
two miles out of Jackson on elk carcasses without ever stepping
on the ground.

The images of struggling elk in that foul season of 1909 are
brutal. Thousands swarmed onto nearby ranches, tearing down
the bulky, fortress-style log fences residents had erected around
their haystacks. Hundreds more poured through the streets of
Jackson, some leaping from snow banks to tear straw loose
from the roofs of barns and sheds, others collapsing, their hides

freezing to the street as they struggled to right themselves, crows and magpies plucking at their eyes. While on any given day the residents of Jackson were at odds with the elk, battling them over graze intended for their cattle, this year it was too much. A meeting was called, the hat was passed, and in a matter of minutes $600 had been raised to buy hay. Residents formed five separate districts across roughly ten miles on either side of the town, each with a local rancher in charge of managing feeding operations. Three years later Congress appropriated $45,000 to buy hay lands northeast of Jackson for winter range; combined with a thousand acres of adjoining public lands, this created a refuge of roughly 2,760 acres. But this too proved woefully inadequate: In the hard winter of 1920 roughly half the elk in the valley perished. Six years later the Isaak Walton League tossed its hat into the ring, purchasing another 1,760 acres adjacent to the existing refuge.

In the early stages of these efforts some predicted the elk would vanish altogether. Reporting in 1898 on the region south of Yellowstone for the Senate, Charles D. Walcott, the Director of the U.S. Geological Survey, painted a grave picture: "It is only a matter of a few years before the winter range will all have been taken, and the game will have followed the buffalo and other large game of Colorado and other sections of the Rockies and the Sierra and Coast ranges and become extinct."

While artificial feeding unquestionably saved the lives of countless elk, it hasn't been without serious drawbacks. For starters, such concentration leaves animals far more vulnerable to the spread of disease. This is of great concern today given the rise of brucellosis (originally brought to the West by domestic cattle) and tuberculosis (37 percent of the cows in the Jackson herd have tested positive); there even exists the threat of chronic wasting disease, which in some respects isn't unlike the mad cow disease that devastated Great Britain's cattle industry in the 1990s. Nor are reproduction rates as high on feeding grounds; in fact, recent studies suggest that cow-calf ratios on the Gros Ventre and National Elk refuges are less than half what they are in free-ranging herds. There have been philosophical concerns as well. As far back as the 1930s, locals were critical of what they perceived as the domestication of wild elk through the feeding program, recounting how refuge animals would often ignore natural foraging opportunities for the chance to take handouts of clover and alfalfa.

If elk have shown a certain knack for responding to the presence of humans—pulling back from unsuitable winter range, swiping hay from protected stacks—they've reserved some of their cleverest tricks for dealing with hunters. The southern Yellowstone herds no longer leave in early fall, as they once did, but remain protected inside the borders of the park until autumn snows force them out. In some seasons the animals begin their southward trek out of Yellowstone after a big snow only to turn around and head back if the weather suddenly improves. Animals that once moved casually out of the park today not only make a beeline for their winter range, but often do so in the thick of night, when no hunters lie in wait. Those leaving Yellowstone heading east for the Greybull River will, on reaching the South Fork of the Shoshone, climb up and over the astonishingly steep flanks of Needle Mountain where neither horse nor hunter is able to follow.

There was a time when elk by the thousand poured south out of the Hawks Rest region toward Turpin Meadow, crossing the highway near Togwotee Pass. (Traveler Charlie Hedrick wrote in 1896 of the season's first big snowstorm letting loose in early November, causing such a massive flow of animals across the pass that he and his companions were forced to hole up in John Cherry's cabin until they passed, like men cowering from a stampede.) Not surprisingly, such movements attracted scores of hunters. Shortly before the close of the 19th century, Charles Walcott of the Geological Survey reported seeing hunting parties camped "on nearly every creek in the large region south of the park, waiting to shoot down the game, which they can freely do under the game laws of Wyoming." If the government failed to prevent such killing in the near future, Walcott argued, then the "rifle and shotgun will as surely exterminate the game as will the destruction of their winter pasture."

As word of these blasting parties spread, it garnered outrage from both hunters and preservationists across the nation, some of whom started calling for a southward expansion of Yellowstone National Park. Well-known biologist George Shiras—at the time a member of the powerful Congressional Committee on Public Lands—pushed hard in 1904 for just such an extension, claiming it was essential to increase both summer and winter ranges for big game. Congressman Frank Mondell of Wyoming, however, also on the Public Lands Committee, assured Shiras that the folks back home were already outraged at the amount of land claimed by national parks and forests, that they "had become rebellious at the idea of any further encroachments on the state lands." In 1905 a compromise was struck. Wyoming created the Teton Game Preserve, which prohibited both hunting and grazing of domestic livestock on a large track of land bordering the southern reaches of the park.

In most places elk hunters were elated. "All sportsmen and all persons interested in game legislation," crooned a writer that year in *Forest and Stream*, "will congratulate the Wyoming Legislature on its wise and far-seeing action." But in 1935, in a move some question to this day, the state decided to scratch all that and open the existing game preserve to hunting. That fall shooters by the hundreds drove their vehicles to upper Spread Creek or lined up along the Buffalo Fork, waiting for the elk to move through lands that the year before had offered safe passage. They were gunned down by the hundreds, in a scene not unlike what had been happening for years elsewhere around the park, some of which was vividly described by naturalist M. P. Skinner in a 1920s article in the *Journal of Mammalogy*.

> Now, you may ask, why should not these hunters have these elk? When a man takes his rifle, hires guides and horses, and goes off into the mountain to hunt elk, he enjoys the change of scene, enjoys matching his skill and endurance against that of his quarry, and later comes home full of renewed life and energy. But if this is the picture you have of these five thousand Yellowstone hunters, dismiss it from your minds. The picture really is a scene in the cold gray morning light when a band of elk, half-starved because the snow covers the forage in the park, starts up the mountain slope across the park boundaries. Nothing happens until the animals have gone a mile beyond the boundary and too far readily to get back again. Then the

slaughterers and the butchers that have been waiting, rush out, surround the hapless elk, and begin shooting with Winchesters and pump guns into the bewildered, huddled band. At times an elk, perhaps wounded, dashes out and through the encircling line. But that encircling line closes in and mercilessly fires into the remaining elk until all have fallen. Sometimes the hunters even continue shooting into the fallen bodies "for fear one will get away." Then all these mighty "sportsmen" rush forward and each claims an elk, saying "this is the one I shot."

As for the elk killed that fall in the former Teton Game Preserve, so horrific was the scene of wounded animals and half-dressed carcasses scattered about that the event came to be known by locals as the Spread Creek Massacre. Well-known artist Archie Teeters captured the scene in a painting called "The Massacre of the Elk," which for years hung in the Jackson Drug Store. The following fall, hunting was dismal, as if the remaining animals had vanished into thin air. Not until well into December did the herds finally start drifting south, crossing the highway near the Blackrock Ranger Station in clusters of several hundred at a time.

For years afterward hunters were hard pressed to find elk south of Yellowstone. So frustrated was the Wyoming Game and Fish Department that in the 1940s they decided to try to draw the animals out onto the national forest, using blocks of salt for bait. The experiment was wrapped in a half-baked theory, which some outfitters cling to even today, that says elk hang out in the park because of a shortage of minerals in the vegetation on the national forest. Never mind that historic records from the 19th and early 20th centuries suggest an abundance of elk on those lands. Seven years after the creation of the Teton Game Preserve, for instance, researchers estimated that about 4,000 elk—roughly 20 percent of the Jackson herd—were spending their summers in Yellowstone, while three times that many were on national forest lands just to the south. Likewise, a Bureau of Biological Survey study in 1915 indicated that the greatest occurrence of elk on summer range was above timberline not just inside Yellowstone, but on high pastures south and east of the park boundaries. "Certainly 100,000 elk could summer comfortably in the Yellowstone Park," the report concluded, "and as many more outside toward the south."

As the decades wore on, the world's finest wildlife biologists could find no evidence of mineral deficiency on the forest. Renowned elk expert Olaus J. Murie said, in his classic 1951 *Elk of North America,* that there were more than enough mineral salts on national forest range, and, furthermore, that the introduction of artificial salting would likely prove useless, if not actually harmful in the long run. Jack Ward Thomas made similar conclusions in his work with biologist Dale E. Toweill. "Salt use by elk," these scientists wrote in 1982, "is primarily a habit formed luxury." After several years of the great salt experiment the only thing state game experts were able to conclude was that there was nothing to conclude. Just the unremarkable news that elk preferred blocks with trace minerals over the more basic calcium-phosphorus variety.

THE MIDDLE OF JULY, and the land of wet is drying fast. Though there are yet great clusters of purple blossoms from wild onion and elephant head in the meadows across from the cabin, their days are clearly numbered. The Yellowstone is dropping six inches a day, warming considerably—good news for those of us whose idea of a Saturday bath is to swim the deep pools. What a week ago was saturated meadow, routinely bogging down horses and mules and sending unwary hikers into muck up to their thighs, can now in most places be walked with water barely coming over the soles of one's boots. Smoke has started drifting into the valley—hints of fires raging from Oregon to southeast Wyoming; most local firefighters are elsewhere, in Colorado on the Hayman fire, or else in Arizona. Not wanting to take any chances, the fire ban stays on in the Teton Wilderness.

Nearly every morning we find lines of fresh wolf tracks courtesy of one or sometimes two animals from the nearby Delta pack—sometimes on the Thorofare Trail itself, just in front of the cabin, but more often along the banks of the river. The signatures are especially clear in the mud bars next to the water, which hold nearly perfect impressions of pads and claws. In the spring of 1995 I was on a project that involved following the original 14 wolves brought in from Canada through the backcountry for nearly a year; members of Delta are descendents from a group of wolves I came to know as well as any other, and as such I've been looking forward to meeting them for a long time. Back then the pack was known as Soda Butte, and parked in the alpha male slot was a mature wolf with a slight cobalt tinge that biologists often referred to as old Blue. Blue was as shy as could be, or so it seemed. Every time the staff would deliver carcasses to the acclimation pen (a half-acre fenced enclosure, where the wolves spent their first nine weeks), he'd make a fast dash into one of the doghouse-like boxes that had been placed there—the only animal ever to make such hasty retreats. One day Blue must've been napping because he didn't get it into gear until the feeding team was already in the pen; in the end he made his usual mad run for the doghouse, brushing the leg of a startled volunteer. Not until nearly nine months after his release did biologists notice him at the front of the chow line on elk kills and, later, calling in other members of the pack like some wise old master.

As the spring of 1995 unfolded, the Soda Butte pack kept moving in wider and wider circles from their release point in the Lamar Valley, eventually ending up in a dramatic slice of canyon along the Stillwater River near Flood Creek. The area had been burned in the 1988 fires and was flush with chokecherry and current, rose and bracken, as well as with sweeps of young aspen and lodgepole pine. In that great green tangle, Blue's mate Number 14 gave birth in early May to what by all appearances was a single female pup. Some questioned her choice of den site, given that just outside those lush thickets was a rocky land, open and exposed, far less abundant with game than other places closer to Yellowstone. Pack members on hunting forays ranged far and wide, sometimes leaving only Blue and his mate to tend the little one, wolf Number 24. But 24 survived, and by the following year she and her family were at a den site on the Lazy EL, a 13,000-acre cattle ranch near Roscoe, Montana.

There are better places to den than on a cattle ranch in Montana. And while the owners of the Lazy EL were more than willing to take a wait-and-see attitude with the Soda Butte wolves, many of their neighbors were not. Thinly veiled threats were tossed out, suggesting that if no one else stepped forward to get rid of those damned things somebody in the neighborhood would. Taking such threats seriously, the Park Service decided in June to relocate the pack to the southeast arm of Yellowstone Lake, placing them in another acclimation pen—this one brought into the backcountry by helicopter—where they remained until the following October. From there the pack headed west to Heart Lake, located in the south-central portion of the park. Then in early spring of 1997, Blue died, mostly from old age. Immediately following his death, his mate, Number 14, began a long, solo run of some 80 miles from the south end of Yellowstone Lake over Pitchstone Plateau, all the way to the Bechler River; after a short stay in that great toss of meadows she finally returned to her pack. But, as wolves sometimes do, she remained alone, and so in neither of the next two springs did the pack see any new pups. Dwindling in size—causing many to fear that their days were numbered—the group made several forays toward Jackson into the National Elk Refuge, but always returned again to the Teton Wilderness and the southern reaches of Yellowstone.

During the warm seasons the entire Thorofare region is a wolf paradise. Just under 20 percent of the massive northern elk herd migrates to this valley to spend the summer, as do thousands of animals from the National Elk Refuge and Gros Ventre feeding grounds. Winter is another story. Indeed, from the very beginning biologists wondered if the Thorofare could support a wolf pack at all, given the mass exodus of elk that occurs immediately following the first big snow. In January 1998, faced with an ongoing struggle for food in the Heart Lake region, Number 14 led the pack eastward into the Thorofare, to a place near Beaverdam Creek. It was here they came muzzle to muzzle with other wolves—a young pack consisting of a pair of alphas and four pups, which researchers had earlier christened the Thorofare pack. In most cases trespassing wolves don't fare all that well when they get into fights in another pack's territory. But the Soda Butte group, now claiming four adults, had the odds in their favor. It was a bloody battle. When the fur finally settled the alpha male of the Thorofare pack was dead, while the alpha female along with one of her pups had been chased into an avalanche chute, where a slide broke loose and killed them both. The remaining pups dispersed. From that moment on, the Thorofare belonged to Soda Butte.

Finally, in April 2000, the pack ended up in the Thorofare going nose to nose with a large moose. Number 14, always quick to lead the action, was killed in the encounter. Though her eldest daughter—that lone little pup born on the Stillwater—had previously gone on to form the Teton pack, unbeknown to researchers a daughter from another litter had already taken over the alpha position, and in that same spring she gave birth to pups near the southeast corner of Yellowstone Lake. With all the original members of Soda Butte gone, the group was renamed the Yellowstone Delta pack. Though 14 may no longer be running these wild hills, I take curious comfort from knowing it was she who first claimed this region as home turf, who so often broke trail for the rest of the pack through countless miles of winter travel, many of her circuits still in use to this day. Wyoming Game and Fish records indicate that only about 200 elk winter in the Thorofare region, which is enough to sustain the pack, but not by much. A wolf in this country works awfully hard for its dinner during the cold months, and that fact has led the Delta pack to become the most far-ranging wolves in the ecosystem. Many a time biologists will climb in the plane and head south on a tracking flight only to never find them, forced to come back and look another day.

Besides their wandering ways, there's another, even more intriguing reason this pack is so hard to keep tabs on. As of this writing the only animal in the entire pack with a collar is the alpha female. Not that others haven't been caught and collared in the past. Rather, they have a strong fondness for chewing the things off each other's necks. "In 2002, we collared five Delta wolves," Park Service wolf project director Doug Smith recalls, sounding a little in awe himself. "All five got chewed off." (The year before had been equally frustrating, when the team collared three wolves only to have two of the collars malfunction. Given that this was the only equipment failure the entire year, it almost leaves a guy wondering if the pack has mastered not only chewing, but electronic sabotage.) "Because 126 is the alpha, the dominant wolf," says Smith, "she doesn't tolerate other members of the pack getting close to her, which is probably the only reason hers is still on." Recently biologists thought they'd solve the problem with a special studded collar, such as the ones worn by bull dogs; it's been used on rare occasions elsewhere, and it always works. Not here. Not with the Delta pack. "They defy our every effort," Smith says with a wide grin.

The mud bars along the river are also rich with signs of beavers and muskrats, moose and pelicans and ducks. And on most mornings, grizzly bear. There are some big bruins wandering these riparian zones each night, sniffing for anything edible, from young birds to eggs to yampa to fish. There are often bear tracks along the edges of the camps as well, though a surprising number of people continue to leave food out—cans of Pepsi and beer, snack cakes and potato chips and bags of Chips Ahoy.

Besides wildlife, most of the human characters have settled into place for the summer as well. Kayla Michael has arrived—aka Lone Eagle Woman—someone I'd long wanted to meet but had no idea how to contact, given that she spends the entire summer drifting alone across some 300 square miles of backcountry, as often as not off the trail. Yet, barely a week after we arrive, here she is standing on our doorstep, wearing ripped jeans, two-dollar knockabout shoes, plastic glasses, and a black Australian-style cowboy hat atop her long blonde hair. We invite her in to eat peanuts and drink Gatorade, and she lights up like a Christmas tree every time we ask anything at all about the park or the wilderness or grizzlies or elk or waterfalls or wolves.

To say Kayla is obsessed with this country would be quite an understatement. In the winter months she works in Jackson, often living in a cut-rate motel or a room in someone's house, all in service of getting back to the Thorofare—if possible in late May, post-holing through two or even three feet of snow, for the simple joy of seeing these meadows ripe with elk and bear and moose, for the chance to spend time here before the circus rolls in and scatters the critters to the winds. For a few sweet weeks hers is a vestige of what famous moose biologist George Shiras found here in 1898. Looking southward toward Bridger Lake and Hawks Rest from a high point in the Thorofare, he wrote that the "country lying between the south end of the lake and the source of the Yellowstone River is the wildest area of its size in the United States," and that it likely contained the "greatest abundance and number of species of animal life wholly unin-fluenced by man."

It was 20 years ago this summer that Kayla first tossed on an 80-pound backpack (which today isn't a shred lighter) and pushed off through the melting snow to the green meadows of Hawks Rest. She's been here nearly every year since, a track record that's left her with an intimate knowledge of the coun-try. Beyond all that, though, she's blessed with unbelievable animal juju. The journal she keeps is solely a record of wildlife encounters and hardly a day goes by that she doesn't spend a fair amount of ink recording them all. She reminds me of a dear woman named Pearl, my next door neighbor when I was a kid. Despite a tough, even at times cruel life, Pearl was in posses-sion of a strange and wonderful piece of fortune. Ever since she was a little girl, her favorite thing in the world was to go fishing, and her particular blessing was that on any given day she could pull in bass and perch and bluegill in quantities that would've impressed Jesus himself. Kayla is like that with wildlife, chalking up more bear sightings, more wolf and elk and moose and beaver encounters in 50 miles of trail than most people could expect in a lifetime of hiking. Maybe like Pearl, somewhere back in her past something cruel fell in on her, but about that I'm only guessing. Because, for all the hours we'll spend together over the coming weeks, there will never be much of any discussion other than the finer points of the world spreading out from the upper Yellowstone and the Thorofare, from Two Ocean Plateau to the Absaroka divide. And, at the same time, this sense that there's never enough hours in the day for her to finish talking about it. On her first visit she stays for three hours before heading back to her camp in the timber south of Bridger Lake—in time for her evening walk, she explains. We sit at the table long after she leaves, our heads about to explode.

Meanwhile, our nearest outfitter neighbor, John Henry Lee (the cowbell king), has by mid-July come calling, as well— riding up early one morning on his white mare with three days of stubble on his chin, steaming mad, like some kind of Roy Rogers gone bad. He's come to take on LaVoy and me for running his horses out of our pasture late the night before and then getting ornery about it with his camp tender. "From now on you've got a problem," he tells us. "I'm the one in charge." It's a pissing match that will continue for weeks. John Henry's a guy trying hard, prone to explosions, a former guide-turned-outfitter running a modest operation in the Teton Wilderness, a small fish in a big pond. A year ago he squared off with outfitter John Winter in a parking lot at Turpin Meadow, going nose to nose over an elk shot by one of John Henry's clients on what Winter claimed was his territory. Each man was backed up by a small band of guides, all of them standing there with hands on their pistols like rival gangs looking for a rumble. Forest Service ranger Cavan Fitzsimmons stumbled onto the scene, looked around, and told the boys he'd come back later, talk with whomever was left standing.

Thrown into the mix too are Forest Service trail crews, who in a land of paper tigers are about as close to champions as you can get. Most are made up of twentysomething men and women who roll into Hawks Rest late in the evening, dark and dusty as chimney sweeps from cutting as many as a hundred trees in a single day—usually burned ones—using nothing but axes and crosscut saws. On their evening ride to the cabin they may stop in at a few camps, make sure food is stored properly and that fires aren't burning during the bans. A few, though, seem unsettled about the task of checking on outfitters, describing the encounters as filled with dodging and double-talk. After reaching the back door of Hawks Rest, they turn out their horses and mules in our pasture (which is why we're trying so hard to protect it from John Henry); picket whomever needs picketing; collapse around the table and consume massive amounts of spaghetti, steak, potatoes, and cookies. Then, at about eleven or twelve o'clock, they head out to lay down in sleeping bags with bug nets laid over their heads and sleep the sleep of the done-in and dog-tired. It's up again a little past dawn to wrangle the horses and mules, eat breakfast, make lunch, reload the stock, and head down the trail to do it all again. Eight days on and six days off.

With the sole exception of Kayla, hardly anyone comes to see us who isn't on a horse. Actually, the reaction to LaVoy and me being here without any stock—let alone the fact that we walked here all the way from Red Lodge—ranges from amusement to pity to something close to contempt. Yesterday a 13-year-old named Julie stopped by the cabin for a visit and was stunned to find out we didn't have horses. "The way I figure it," she said on her way out the door, "God wouldn't have made horses if he didn't intend for us to ride them." He made legs too, I offered, but the point was clearly lost. Meanwhile, this afternoon Dick from Worland, Wyoming, camped just south of Bridger Lake, sipped on a Bud Light and wondered out loud why the Forest Service would hire backpackers as cabin tenders, as if all we could offer was to sit on the porch and eat granola. I'm taken aback at first, half-tempted to tell him about John Colter. Arguably Wyoming's favorite hero, he's the guy who after two years with Lewis and Clark turned his back on the chance for civilization to return to the Rockies for several more years. On most of his journeys he wasn't a horseman at all, but a backpacker. A simple, gnarly pedestrian who walked thousands of miles in every season, carrying with him a stash of beads, awls, and vermilion as presents for the Indians. In the end, though, I decide to save my breath. Dick seems about as likely to buy that story as he is to reach into his panniers and offer me a Perrier.

One of the more frequent visitors—and among the most amiable—is Dann Harvey, in the Thorofare for the summer with about a dozen 12- to 16-year-olds from the Wyoming Wilderness Academy. Their provisions are stored in the tack room, and on any given day several kids will thunder up on horseback to retrieve more oatmeal or spaghetti sauce, macaroni and cheese or handfuls of candy. Part of the day the group spends working on trails or cutting poles for fence, cleaning up trash from other camps, pruning back the small lodgepole pine trees that keep crowding the trails in the wake of the 1988 burns. The rest of their time goes to studying animal tracks, figuring out maps, or recording wildlife sightings, especially bear and elk, information fed to Wyoming Game and Fish. Then, of course, there's fishing and swimming in the Yellowstone, floating down the river laying on logs, pretending to be alligators. For some reason the Delta wolf pack seems especially fond of the kids of the Wyoming Wilderness Academy, having on several occasions parked themselves late at night on a trail not 40 yards from their tents to let loose with a chorus of howls.

The kids blossom before our eyes. Which is a fine thing, given how tough most of their lives are back home: parents in prison, addicted moms and alcoholic dads, survivors of abuse, some living with relatives and others in group homes. Yet through all that they've somehow managed to forge an internal ballast deep and weighty enough to keep them upright. A good example of these kids, Dann tells me over coffee one morning, is a 14-year-old boy named Tom. "Dad's in jail and mom's an alcoholic, a prostitute. This kid goes down and signs himself up for school, enrolls himself in the right classes, gets up every single morning and does what he needs to do. Exactly the kind of kid who falls through the cracks when it comes to getting any kind of helping hand."

Dann says that over 18 years he's seen kids with behaviors that used to get people's attention get pushed to the bottom of the heap. The system is overwhelmed, he explains, pointing out that in California alone there's a directory nearly two inches thick filled with the names of boys and girls who just need someplace to go. "When you've got that kind of need, kids pretty much have to be criminals to have anything made available to them," he says. Wyoming Wilderness Academy depends on teachers and principals to recommend boys or girls who might really enjoy a summer on horseback in the wilds, then beats the bushes to find corporate sponsors to get them here.

Last but not least in the Hawks Rest scene are the park rangers. In particular, Bob Jackson. The passionate—some might say possessed—action figure hero so much in the news today. Both for his fight with outfitters against salting elk, but no less for his ongoing brawl with the National Park Service, which is locked in a nearly epic march of folly, trying to stuff a sock into Bob's mouth for the unpardonable sin of breaking the chain of command to take his antisalting crusade to the press. Of all the characters in the Thorofare, few deserve ink more than Bob.

CHAPTER FIVE

*T*HERE IS IN THE GREEN FOLDS OF THE MIDWEST, tucked between the cornfields and the soybeans, squatting on what was once a broad flush of prairie at the end of State Highway 55, a town of 850 or so called Seymour, Iowa. Those in search of gas or a gallon of milk or a slice of pizza can get all that and more at Casey's General Store, while visitors looking to spend the night will do no better than to head straight for the Seymour Bed and Breakfast over on Lee Street. The faithful (and there are a lot of faithful here) have no shortage of places to worship, including the First Baptist Church on Wall Street, the Assembly of God on Fifth, and, a block off State Highway 55, the United Methodist Church of Seymour. Any of which would be more than happy to tend your soul. Some years back the Methodists were feeling a bit ragged and run down, ill at ease with the fact that their church had grown, well, a bit dowdy. After considering the matter at length, some of the trustees thought it might be best to do what the Millerton Methodist Church had done: replace the old sanctuary with a Morton building, which had, after all, worked just fine for a lot of the local farmers who used them as tool sheds. Still others suggested the cover-up method, trimming out the old windows and putting that nifty looking sparkly texture over the cracks in the ceiling. But one young fellow, an enthusiastic man in his late forties, had an altogether different notion. As far as he was concerned, it was impossible to improve on what was already there. He had a special way of looking, able to see beyond cracks and faded coats of lacquer to virgin heart pine lying underneath. He was a man who believed in restoration.

Restoration, though, takes a lot of effort, and this was after all a bunch of volunteers. On any given day you might get a lot of praying for success, but let's face it, it's darned hard to get even a handful of people willing to commit to the actual labor such projects require. Luckily this fellow had not only the gift of restoration, but also of persuasion—in some ways as much as the preacher himself, which some say has to do with the fact that preaching had run in his family for generations. The first order of business was to mobilize the women. That was easy, he says; in no time at all they'd assembled in the center of the sanctuary and rolled up their sleeves to begin the arduous task of stripping old finish from existing boards. Next he gathered the men, the farmers, told them to bring in their tools—orbital sanders, belt sanders—and oh, they liked the sound of that. He placed the men up in the balcony above the women because, he says, in truth men work real hard for an hour and then they get to talking, forget all about the job at hand. He figured that if the men were always looking down on the women, who pretty much kept focused on the task all the way through to quitting time, they might just work a little more, whether out of guilt or dishonor or even just plain inspiration, who can say for sure.

One day the editor of the *Seymour Herald* got wind of the project, showed up on-site with notepad and camera. That one newspaper article brought in other church members—perhaps lured by the chance of future fame—who'd been standing on the sidelines; indeed, the next time the editor showed up there were a lot more volunteers, close to a hundred. The scaffolding was ratcheted higher, even though it probably didn't need to be, and the men were up there working just as hard as the women. To make a long story short, the place turned out beautifully. Months after the project was finished, you could look off to the end of a given pew during Sunday service and see some farmer, dressed in an ill-fitting blue suit, leaning forward with the palm of his hand on the wood pillar next to him, feeling the smoothness of the sanding job. One of the last things those people of the United Methodist Church of Seymour did at the end of the restoration was to hang a plaque out in the foyer, thanking that fine young man who had the vision and courage to take on the restoration in the first place. "With special gratitude," it says, "to Bob Jackson."

Some thousand miles to the west, in the remote reaches of the Teton Wilderness, there is no such plaque. And even if there was, more than likely it wouldn't be inscribed with the kind of sentiment you'd be inclined to hang in a church. Indeed, behind the Wyoming Game and Fish cabin just south of the park boundary is a two-seater outhouse, one hole larger than the other, and for a long time the bigger hole had a hand-lettered sign over it that said "Park Rangers"—a jab meant entirely for Bob.

A couple weeks after arriving at Hawks Rest, LaVoy and I step out to do a bit of neighboring, heading out around four o'clock with packs loaded for an overnight, making a three-mile trek along the east side of the upper Yellowstone meadows, fording a thigh-deep Thorofare Creek, to join Bob for dinner. It's a beautiful walk—the meadows glowing in the afternoon sun, the trail seasoned with the tracks of bears and wolves. The smoke has cleared somewhat, allowing us fine views of that brilliant commotion of rock rising behind the Thorofare cabin that forms the fingers of The Trident. Near the creek in a ribbon of willow we hoot and holler a bit, try to telegraph our location to any bears that might be rummaging about. But for most of the trek we're quiet, savoring the chortle of sandhill cranes overhead, breathing in the earthy smell of the meadows, the pepper of pine.

The Thorofare cabin looks bright, clean, well tended. The kitchen is wrapped in white wainscoting and old spice cans from the 1920s, each filled with pepper and basil and oregano, line the walls; absolutely everything is in order, right down to the arrangement of food in the cabinets. A beautiful black-and-silver wood cookstove—brought in by helicopter from Enis, Montana—sits along the west wall; made by the Malleable Stove Mfg. Company of South Bend, Indiana, it sports such finery as warming bins and a hot water reservoir. Bob points to the table in the corner and says he isn't happy with the red-apple motif on the cloth, that the red-checkered oilcloth that used to be there went a lot better with the decor. The fir floor seems fairly new, and as the evening sun drops lower in the sky the red in the wood glows ever brighter.

On a bench on the east side of the kitchen is a combination cooler and water filter. On this matter, and on this matter alone, have we got Bob one better at Hawks Rest, what with our dandy spring-fed kitchen sink. He fairly swoons with the thought of running a water line into his quarters from a nearby spring creek, but while that might have been possible several years ago, given how his fortunes have soured it seems unlikely to happen anytime soon. Some in the Park Service are already twitter-pated about the elevated tent platform he erected behind the main quarters, as well as the outside shower he's constructing in the woods with the help of an engineering friend. Located some 50 yards south of the cabin, the shower is somewhat bigger than a phone booth, consisting of three-foot-high panels topped by screen walls. On top of the frame are two black metal drums, each with a hose running out of the bottom leading to a homemade showerhead, the flow of water controlled by valves. Hot water is created by placing a coil of tubing—a piece looking something like a part from a still—into the adjacent fire pit, then building a fire around it to create a head of pressure that circulates the water through one of the barrels. Before dinner we help Bob make a few adjustments, struggle to stop leaks in the system by cutting out and securing rubber gaskets onto the fittings at the bottom of each drum.

As for the barn out back, the oldest backcountry structure in the park, this also wears signs of Jackson's handiwork. He's built cabinets and tool chests, taken an adze to level and smooth the four-inch-thick pine floorboards. The building itself has been raised and two additional logs placed underneath, offering better headroom underneath the grain mow. An open shed is affixed to the outside where horses can be tied and shod, and the structure includes a hand-peeled log feed trough carved by chain saw. The corrals are in incredibly good shape, right down to a perfectly hung gate (I can't stand a dragging gate, Bob tells us). Saddles get laid across the massive top rail, and soon to come are feeding stations that can be tipped to empty them of pine needles and other debris.

The room next to the kitchen in the main cabin is also covered in wainscoting, though stained darker, making it feel more like a den or a library. It holds two cots, several rows of books on topics ranging from wildlife to the Assiniboine Indians of northern Montana, and a bulky tabletop park radio, which Bob uses to make his daily check-ins, a routine that he begins, without fail and to the horror of some, by announcing to the dispatcher that "everything is A-OK at El Rancho Thorofare."

The tour finished, it's time to get down to dinner. Despite all our company, LaVoy and I have been living in what feels like slow motion for several weeks, so it's alarming to see a freshly shaved Jackson scooting around the kitchen floor of the cabin as if on roller skates, shuffling pans, dropping into the root cellar and then up and out again, double-timing to finish off a pot of buffalo spaghetti. A few mosquitoes are whining inside the cabin, and every now and then Bob halts his frantic maneuvers long enough to smash a couple with big claps of his thick fingers. So great is his energy, so sweeping his gestures, I'm half afraid he may accidentally toss the entire meal through the kitchen window, where it would no doubt be inhaled by one of his faithful horses, which when they aren't staring in the window at us are tromping across the front porch, sniffing for goodies in LaVoy's backpack. Bob talks as fast as he moves. Charged with making a cheesecake for dessert, I soon discover that turning the crank of the hand mixer at roughly the pace of his speech approximates the high setting on an electric mixer. He pauses only long enough to swallow; the rest of the time he's cajoling, explaining, telling fragments from a raft of stories, leading us as if by halter to reveal the issue that's brought him such enormous helpings of both fame and loathing.

Bob's current predicament began unfolding about four years ago, in 1998. It was then he gave to his supervisor a five-page report he'd written called "Grizzly Mortality in the Thorofare," based, he explains, on more than two decades of observing outfitter activity along the southern border of Yellowstone. The nut of the paper's argument is the claim that certain hunting practices are creating a situation in that region of the backcountry not unlike the "old-time garbage dumps of Yellowstone National Park, with abnormally high concentrations of bears." This, he says, could lead to increased aggression, and ultimately to a habituation of the grizzly, which in turn would place both the bear and humans at risk of injury or death. The reasons for these high concentrations of bears are varied, the report explains, but all are based on a growing supply of meat on the ground during hunting season: first, from an increase in the number of hunters; second, from the illegal use of salt to draw elk out of the park and hold them in the wilderness; and, finally, from the increasingly common practice of quick quartering elk, which can mean 50 or 60 pounds of edible fare left on the ground for scavengers.

Plain and simple, there's a lot of merit to Bob's portrayal of what's going on in the Thorofare. Even so, it's not easy to say what the real impact of such practices might be. One of the oldest-operating outfitters in the area freely admits that salting "holds more elk outside Yellowstone." And while bull elk can't exactly be said to congregate around those salts, the fact that the

sites bring more of them into the area means, of course, that more
will be shot during hunting season. That, in turn, means more meat
lying on the ground, which could certainly lead to a higher
concentration of bears. Furthermore, potential problems could
well be more acute because of the practice of quick quartering,
which adds substantially to the quantity of meat available to
bears. (Curiously, Wyoming Hunter Education Director Helen
McCracken maintains there's a requirement for hunters to "take
all edible meat." But in truth the law requires only that you take
the backstrap and quarters, and that opens the door to dis-
carding all flesh on the rib cage, the 30 to 40 pounds of meat on
the neck, and, because quarters aren't specifically defined, por-
tions of those as well.) Wyoming is currently the only state in
the region that allows that kind of carcass dressing—yet another
indication, many say, of the powerful influence of the outfitting
industry, which has long complained that taking out all the
meat would present a hardship, requiring extra manpower and
more pack animals. While Bob Jackson may be best known as
a staunch opponent of salting, when this fracas began quick quartering was his biggest concern. It was the media, he says, that
were especially fond of the salting angle.

Jackson claims quick quartering adds to the likelihood of
bears showing up in the first place—that gut piles alone were tra-
ditionally cleaned up quickly by other scavengers, leaving so little behind it wasn't worth the bears' efforts. But that's uncertain.
According to a study done in 1986, when the practice of outfitters salting along the southern border was very much in its
infancy, sport hunting around the perimeter of Yellowstone was
estimated to be leaving roughly 500 tons of flesh, organs, and
bones as a potential food source for bears. Quick quartering aside,

most biologists think bears know full well where the hunting hot spots are, and that in fact it's the stronger-smelling gut pile that serves as a scent marker for drawing them into a given area in the first place. Besides that, these days they rely not just on their noses but on their ears, often running toward the sound of guns. Still, it does seem close to ludicrous that you can be cited by both the state and the Forest Service for leaving a candy bar sitting out at your campsite, while it's no problem to leave 50 pounds of meat lying on the ground.

It's also questionable whether or not bears become more aggressive as they concentrate. Grizzlies cluster around food sources all the time—during cutworm moth feeding, at streams during spawning runs, for decades at the dumps, for hundreds of years at buffalo jumps. Rather than the bears becoming overly aggressive, there tends to unfold a strict social hierarchy, with the largest and strongest getting the choicest opportunities. Furthermore, just because a grizzly is on a carcass doesn't necessarily mean it will rip a hiker's head off. Yellowstone bear biologist Kerry Gunther has been doing carcass studies for 20 years, and in that time he's come upon a lot of bears on elk carcasses. "Typically a bear will stand on a carcass and dare you to take it from him, but if you don't surprise it, if you back off the same way you came, he'll let you out. Where we've had problems is people stumbling across a carcass and then trying to detour around it, only to come across a bear in his day bed."

Bob's claim that a lot of conflicts could be avoided simply by the proper tending of meat is irrefutable. It would seem only common sense to remove everything from a kill site right away, either by hanging it, carrying it out of the backcountry, or taking it back to camp—an approach that's bound to help keep hunters and bears separated. Yet most outfitters don't do this. Some tell me it would be dangerous. Elk are often shot at twilight, they explain, and packing them out would mean being out after dark, when the grizzly danger factor goes up considerably. Of course, most outfitters are riding trail in pitch dark every morning anyway, though admittedly not with carcasses on board. On the other hand, not carrying the meat out right away can be a perfect management tool for the lazy. Elk shot at twilight almost always have their racks and capes taken right away. When the guide and his hunter return the next morning, though, it's common to find the carcass buried with a bear sitting on top of it—a situation that rather conveniently eliminates any need to worry about taking out the meat. Some hunters may be disappointed to have lost their steaks, but in truth most don't hire guides to take them into the Thorofare to fill their freezers with meat.

Back in 1998 no one was really sure about the veracity of Bob's claims, and they still aren't. Nevertheless, at the time it was released, "Grizzly Mortality in the Thorofare" earned Jackson a hearty pat on the back. Supervisor John Lounsbury recommended the paper be passed around to various people from the Forest Service, Park Service, Wyoming Game and Fish, and U.S. Fish and Wildlife, who were about to gather for a so-called pre-hunt meeting, an annual affair to coordinate management and enforcement priorities for the coming hunting season. According to Bob, after reading his report, Rick Hudson, the highest ranking member of the Forest Service present, told the group he hoped there wasn't a tape recorder playing, "because this report is 100 percent right." No doubt one reason Hudson was glad for the lack of tape recorders is because Jackson doesn't exactly paint a flattering portrait of outfitters. And in Wyoming, slamming out-fitters is a messy business.

These days Bob is thought of by many in the park as a heretic—a guy who short-circuited the chain of command for the chance to waltz this issue under the bright lights of the media. He swears that's not how it happened. When that report came out in 1998, he explains, "the extent of my exposure to media was giving slide shows about Yellowstone to Rotary Clubs in Iowa. Every request for information I forwarded to the public affairs office." He goes on to say that every person at that pre-hunt meeting took a copy of the report, and it was one of them—or someone in their offices—who leaked it to the press. However it happened, the press got it all right, and the first fire was lit by the *Jackson Hole News* in September of that same year. Curiously, in that article Jackson is not only quoted as saying these are his own personal views and not those of the Park Service, but it's clear that others are in his court. Park bear biologist Kerry Gunther credits him for making some good points, acknowl-edging that "fires and salting and gut piles have concentrated bears—drawn [them] to that area." Meanwhile, the park's pub-lic affairs office called Jackson's work informative, saying how much administrators depended on long-term seasonals to keep them informed about issues in remote locations.

As media attention grew, the outfitters displayed the arro-gance of the untouchable. Despite the fact that it had been illegal to use salt in the Teton Wilderness since 1991, in that same *Jackson Hole News* article Harold Turner of Triangle X Outfitters acknowledged that he used it in his operation (a statement he would later deny), calling it "a good management tool." Two years after this interview, after the state of Wyoming had finally passed a law against salting, he acknowledged to Hal Herring of *Bugle* magazine that in most years some outfitters were still placing salt, "but since the Forest Service prohibition, [most of them] don't talk about it much." It helped concentrate elk back in the 1950s, Turner said, and it helps now—"especially given the fact that we've got a wolf pack in there scattering them out nowadays." (An intriguing aside to this latter comment is that Harold Turner's brother John, former director of the U.S. Fish and Wildlife Service from 1989 to 1993, has on at least one occasion taken credit for making wolf reintroduction possible in the first place.) In the same article, Lynn Madsen of Yellowstone Outfitters told *Bugle* that "sometimes we do hunt over the salts, especially with guys who can't handle the real thing, can't take the rough country." I'll hear more or less the same comment over and over again this summer from guides throughout the northern reaches of the wilderness, most of whom say the "salts are for the fat guys."

Throughout the year following his "Grizzly Mortality in the Thorofare" report, Jackson remained somewhat of a favored child with many in Yellowstone. In August 1999, administrative biologists Wayne Brewster and Glen Plumb seemed enthusiastic about pursuing the link between salting and bear problems, actually making a trip to the Thorofare to ride the boundary with Jackson and look for salts. "Thanks for sharing your hard-earned wisdom," Plumb wrote in the Thorofare cabin logbook on August 6. "It won't be long before I see you again"—a comment Jackson says relates Plumb's intention to come back with biologists to begin placing GPS coordinates on the major salt sites. Others say Plumb was merely blowing smoke, offering a quick kudo with no intention of ever following up. Either way, it was the last thumbs-up Bob would get.

Two weeks after Plumb's visit, Mark Marschall informed Jackson that the biologists had changed their thinking, that salting was no longer an issue. Jackson says that in late September of that same year, in a meeting at the Thorofare cabin, U.S. Fish and Wildlife agent Dominic Domenici told him he wouldn't be able to support his position in an upcoming interview with *Los Angeles Times* reporter Frank Clifford. "He said to Sharon McGee earlier that evening that he basically agreed with me," claims Bob, "but that he wasn't in a position to say so." The following month Wyoming Game and Fish called salting a nonissue, a position they more or less still hold today. Rick Hudson of the Bridger-Teton National Forest—the guy who Bob claims expressed being grateful there were no tape recorders running at that prehunt meeting—was backpedaling fast, telling a reporter from the *Jackson Hole News* that most outfitters have stopped salt baiting since the regulations went into effect nearly a decade ago. "We have heard the accusations of [outfitter Tory] Taylor and others, but we have been presented with no information where any of our outfitters have actually been caught (with salt) for the intent of baiting." Bob Jackson was being cut loose. As Dan Meyer, general counsel for Public Employees for Environmental Responsibility, would tell the *Los Angeles Times* two years later, "The bottom line is Bob has walked between the outfitters and their loaf of bread."

Leaving aside for a minute the merits of Jackson's arguments, or even whether or not he was seeking attention from the media, what's extraordinary is how the Park Service stumbled in their efforts to distance themselves from him. It would've been a simple matter, after all, to transfer him out of the Thorofare to the front country, turn him into a ticket taker at the East

Entrance station, claim his vast experience was of better use where more people could interact with him. But that didn't happen. Jackson's annual evaluation for his work that season, prepared by Pete Dalton in the fall of 2000, reads like a letter from a proud schoolmaster. According to Dalton, Jackson "achieved all his critical elements in the areas of visitor protection and services, resource protection and education, collateral duties and special projects." Bob was further observed to be outstanding in his public contacts and assistance he provided to the public, in particular stock users. Dalton says Bob's contacts with outfitters operating outside the park, in the Bridger-Teton National Forest, were "very professional, polite and appropriate"—that he's shown himself "to be a valuable asset to the visitor and resource protection operation for the Lake Sub-District Area, as well as the Park." Still more kudos were handed off for all the work he did cleaning, repairing, and rehabilitating cabins outside the Thorofare—an effort above the standard, greatly appreciated. "It should be noted," Dalton concluded, "that in the spring of 2000 Bob received the federal employee of the year award presented to him by the Greater Yellowstone Coalition, who honored him performing his job as a National Park Service Backcountry Ranger at Yellowstone."

The following year's evaluation, covering Bob's season that ran June 4 through October 7, when the salting issue seemed to be getting out of control, suggests an absurd level of decline. Suddenly Jackson is no longer achieving several important criteria under his performance plan. He fails at collateral duties and skills, at soundness of judgment and decision, and at effectiveness of communications. The same guy who was polite and professional in his communications the year before was now failing at everything from quality and timeliness of service to courtesy. "Last year Bob received an overall rating of achieved," wrote Dalton, "however after closer review of past performance evaluations and site visits to Bob's work areas (Thorofare) I have observed a pattern of work habits that has not achieved basic level of acceptable performance."

After a quarter century as a seasonal, Bob was told that from now on he must "submit request two weeks in advance for permission for guest, family and friends to use any of the backcountry patrol cabin facilities." (Bob says he was later denied permission to have his kids visit the Thorofare cabin—kids who grew up there—told that he was there to work, not to entertain visitors.) He was further instructed that "all media, news, reporter, journalist and interview requests must be directed to the public affairs office," that he was "not to represent the NPS on any issues related to the Park or Park Service without prior approval of the Chief Ranger's office." Prior to every patrol his supervisor would prepare a plan, and any deviation from it would have to be approved in advance. "In incidents where pre-approval could not be obtained, written documentation must be submitted to your supervisor listing the reasons for actions taken." Bob has a lot of good knowledge, skills, and abilities, concluded Dalton. "However, these attributes are overshadowed by established poor work habits and work relationship with those that we count on to get the job done."

All of that, though, pales in comparison to a now-famous gag order written on August 28, 2001. "Bob Jackson is not authorized to speak to the media while on government time," it begins. "He is not authorized to speak to the media as a representative of Yellowstone National Park Service at any time."

Then in a flash of true madness the authors try to plug every conceivable loophole, ignoring altogether the small matter of the First Amendment. "On his days off and outside the park, he can talk to the media, but is not authorized to express opinions regarding Yellowstone National Park, the National Park Service or about anything he does in his official capacity with the National Park Service. During any media contact, he is not authorized to be in uniform and must make it clear that he is not representing the National Park Service. He is only allowed to give factual information about his position even though he is off duty." Golden boy Bob Jackson, the ranger who for years was celebrated by big rollers in Mammoth, invited to special parties where he could be counted on to entertain dignitaries with stories about catching poachers in the remote wilds of southern Yellowstone, was damaged goods.

In the fall of 2001 Bob would later write an intriguing letter to acting Park Superintendent Frank Walker, focusing on what to him seemed like flat-out paranoia.

> I feel the reason my supervisors didn't allow me to stay in the backcountry was the fear of journalists sneaking back there to interview me. I was caught in a catch-22—the park thought I was initiating contact with all kinds of media if I was in the front country on my days off, and they also thought I would conduct "illegal" interviews if I was allowed to stay in the backcountry. They even shared descriptions of backpackers who asked "suspicious" sounding questions to see if they matched up with known journalists' physical

descriptions. I think some of the people making all those decisions about my weekly duty assignments have been watching too many detective movies. My supervisors spent a lot of time strategizing how to keep an imaginary press away from me, and Thorofare went untended.

Later this summer, on the trail with Jackson, I'll hear him describe yet another long series of nuisance requirements being handed down by his superiors, as if they had a hazing campaign going on, trying to see how much he could take. "You'll find out," he will mutter, mostly to himself. "You'll find out." No matter what side of the fence you come down on with Bob, it's hard to deny he's had an affect. "Ten years ago," explains one private Wyoming hunter, "I saw salts all over in Thorofare Creek, but that dropped drastically when Bob started raising a stink. It still goes on, but now it's more in out of the way places." That said, the hunter says he figures some outfitters are just waiting, biding their time for two or three years until Bob is gone and they can start it up all over again. He might be right, considering that right now Wyoming Game and Fish (and to a lesser extent, the U.S. Fish and Wildlife Service) is spending far more effort trying to refute Bob's claims about the effects of salting on grizzlies than they ever spent enforcing existing laws against the practice.

CHAPTER SIX

*W*HILE THE STATE MAY HAVE BEEN PLAYING around with using salt to draw elk out of the park to improve hunting as far back as the 1940s, most outfitters didn't jump into the act until much later; according to former District Ranger Don Hooper the practice wasn't common until the 1980s. "When I first came onto the forest in 1961," Hooper recalls, "over near Fox Park, down along the Snake River on the east side of Big Game Ridge, you could see dozens of elk trails going down to a natural salt lick, a mile and a half or so from the forest boundary." Hooper recalls there being little evidence of artificial salting by outfitters—an opinion seconded by former backcountry ranger Merv Coleman, who says during his hitch at Fox Park in the mid-1960s he can't recall coming across a single salting site anywhere in the wilderness.

Then, in the summer of 1985, on a pack trip with his son, Hooper noticed that the web of elk trails leading to that natural salt lick on the Snake River wasn't being used nearly to the degree it'd been 20 years earlier. Two days later, riding near the present site of the Wyoming Game and Fish cabin on Thorofare Creek, some 200 yards south of the Yellowstone border, Hooper found what he thinks is the reason why. "There was this big area, all tramped out, about 30 feet in diameter. It had a depression right in the center, almost two feet deep. And right in the middle were two salt blocks." Toward the end of his trip, along Atlantic Creek, Hooper ran across outfitter Randy Haecker, who was in the area for the opening of moose season. The two men started talking, Haecker having no idea that Hooper was an employee of the Forest Service.

"Saw some salt blocks out near the park boundary," Hooper offered.

"Yeah," replied Haecker. "All of us are putting those out now."

Why outfitters started salting more frequently in the 1980s is something that even the outfitters don't seem to know for sure. Backcountry ranger Cavan Fitzsimmons speculates it may be a reflection of what was starting to happen then in the culture at large, a smear on hunting left by the so-called decade of greed. "There used to be a lot of out-of-state hunters happy just being out here. But in the 1980s people started coming more with the idea of getting results. They wanted trophies." Outfitter Richard Clark makes a similar point, saying that today there are basically two questions on the minds of most hunting clients: "What's your kill ratio?" and "Can I get a trophy elk?"

At the same time corporate America was wallowing in merger fever, so too were many outfitting companies in the western forests being bought out, not just by more powerful neighbors, but by wealthy people from out of state. And these

newcomers were often men who expected results. The days of
the casual outfitter—working most of the year as a plumber in
Cody, or managing an auto parts store in Riverton—were fast
coming to an end. The truly weird part of all this is that the factor
most responsible for a change in fortunes, enabling trophy-
minded hunters to get their fix and outfitters to build reputations
on it, were the fires of 1988. The same gigantic burns that many
locals cursed the Park Service and Forest Service for allowing to
happen in the first place not only resulted in better forage, but
also removed tree cover, allowing hunters to achieve remarkable
levels of success. Logbook entries by patrol rangers during
the late 1970s and early '80s talk of outfitter success rates in the
Thorofare region between 30 and 40 percent. By the early
1990s those same outfitters were bragging in their brochures and
outdoor magazine ads of kill rates over 90 percent. Indeed,
those fires helped hunters around much of Yellowstone boast
the highest success rates of any public elk hunting lands in the
country. Outfitter Lynn Madsen recently told a wolf biologist that
he didn't much care about the wolf reintroduction at the moment,
but that as soon as his success rates started going down, somebody would need to start knocking down wolves. Yet Madsen
wasn't here in the days of 30 to 40 percent success rates, common for years before wolves returned to the ecosystem.

That experience along Atlantic Creek made Don Hooper
decide to launch what was in fact the first campaign against salting, a torch he carried well into retirement. "I remember the
regional forester meeting with me on my last day of work,
telling me that yes, salting was something they were going to take
care of. But it was just eye wash." In the same way today Bob
Jackson earns the wrath and threats of outfitters, Hooper was

getting it with both barrels all through the nineties. "I needed a flak jacket and a helmet to go back there," he says. "There were comments made, of course never with any witnesses around— talk about how if I didn't watch it my wife was going to become a widow."

While Jackson has centered his fight against salting on potential threats to grizzly bears, Hooper took a more basic approach—the plain fact that salting was against the provisions of the Wilderness Act. To begin with, he argued, the Wilderness Act is prohibitive rather than permissive, which means those activities not expressly authorized simply aren't allowed. Salting is not only unauthorized, but there's a specific provision in the act against controlling the movement of wildlife. Yet Hooper's calls to action were totally ignored. In a chronic case of double-speak, Bridger-Teton Forest Supervisor Brian Stout acknowledged in a letter of August 1988 that the Wilderness Act prohibits direct control of wildlife, but went on to claim that salting to encourage elk redistribution "is not control." And besides, Stout maintained, elk aren't hunted directly over the salt blocks themselves, but rather the salt was merely to better distribute the animals, "thereby providing a quality wilderness recreation experience for hunters." Reading on, and largely between the lines, it appears that Stout was leaning on the old theory that elk are absent from the forest because of mineral deficiencies in the soil, that by providing salt the outfitters were correcting a deficiency of the land itself. The only problem is that at the time outfitters weren't using mineral blocks at all, but plain old salt.

At the same time, the chief game warden of the Wyoming Game and Fish Department pointed out that salt was being placed throughout Wyoming "because this is a livestock producing state, and the salt blocks are very much available to any of the wildlife wishing to use it." Never mind that cattle and sheep weren't even allowed on the northern reaches of the Teton Wilderness.

Despite being a thorn in the side of many, not long after his retirement Hooper received an interesting invitation. There was to be a field trip to the northern Teton Wilderness in the wake of the 1988 fires, a management coordination meeting including representatives from the Bridger-Teton and Targhee National Forests, Grand Teton and Yellowstone National Parks, the Wyoming Game and Fish Department, outfitters, and biologists from the Universities of Wyoming and Montana. One of the items on the agenda was salting. But when the party got to the farthest reaches of the backcountry, Hooper once again found out what he was up against. Out of 21 people present, he was the only one who thought salting was an issue even worth talking about.

"Look," offered outfitter Don Turner of Triangle X, "it's better we draw in the elk and kill them [on the forest], instead of having to do it in Grand Teton Park or on the elk refuge." A remark referring to the fact that, in order to control elk populations, limited hunting is allowed both in the park and on the refuge.

"Ordinarily I'd agree with you," Hooper recalls saying. "But this is a wilderness area. And a wilderness area is a different breed of land. If this was just regular national forest I wouldn't care if you put out bait for all the slob hunters you wanted to bring in, and all the unprofessional outfitters who wanted to take them."

One member of the group asked the outfitters exactly how they used the salts, and Hooper says Turner claimed they never actually hunted over them, that they were simply an enticement for the elk to stay out of the park. To which the recently retired Hooper—at this point obviously enjoying a certain freedom of speech—offered a sour comeback. "Yeah," he said. "And ducks don't fart underwater, either." To his credit Randy Haecker, the outfitter Hooper met on the trail near Atlantic Creek several years earlier, offered what may have been a more honest response: "We go in there and if our hunters find an elk on the salt block, we zap 'em."

Near the end of the field trip Don Turner turned to Hooper and asked a question the Turners would be no less eager to ask Bob Jackson today. "Why don't you take up some kind of hobby and stay the hell out of this wilderness?"

"I'm willing to do that," he replied. "Instead of the salting issue, how about I start spending all my time on getting outfitter caches removed?" (This was a reference to a prohibition in the Wilderness Act forbidding permanent structures and long-term storage of gear in backcountry sites—both of which are common yet today.) Hooper smiles at the memory of it. "People thought we were going to come to blows."

The Forest Service ultimately did rise to the occasion, at least on paper, forbidding salting as of 1991—an effort led in large part by deputy regional forester Bob Joselyn. "But [a lot of] outfitters never did abide by it," Hooper says. "They'd leave salt where they camped, put it out for their horses and just leave it there. And you could always find blocks in the trees, next to some of the meadows where they'd left the salt blocks before. The Forest Service never did anything, claiming they didn't have the manpower to deal with it."

In the late 1990s, the Wyoming Wildlife Federation, a group composed mostly of private hunters, took on the salting issue as a sportsmen's cause. "It's a fair chase hunting issue," says former federation director Kim Floyd. "Salting is nothing but baiting wild game animals. We tried to get the Bridger-Teton National Forest involved, we tried to work with rangers from Yellowstone National Park. And we had a lot of opposition from the outfitters." Ironically, the state legislator who introduced the bill that finally made salting illegal was Republican legislator Marlene Simon, who had no particular interest in either the Teton Wilderness or Yellowstone. As a rancher and outfitter living in northeast Wyoming, Simon had grown tired of outfitters on lands adjacent to her ranch using corn to bait whitetail deer and, in the process, screwing up her own hunting. The Wyoming Wildlife Federation simply pushed to have salt tacked onto the definition of bait in Simon's bill against artificially luring wildlife.

Forget for a minute notions that salting might impact grizzly bears, à la Bob Jackson. Forget even the greater certainty that such practice is not only against the tenets of the Wilderness Act, but prohibited by both forest regulation and Wyoming state law. What you're left with is the damage such practices cause to the image of hunting at large. There was a time, after all, when Wyoming was so committed to the ideals of good sportsmanship that they placed quips about hunter ethics in their annual reports. The final page of the 1918 Report of the State Game Warden, for example, went so far as to include Zane Grey's "The American Sportsman's Creed." "Obey the laws of state and nation," advises Grey. "Work for better laws, and uphold the law enforcing authorities. I want my boy and his comrades and the boys of the future to receive this heritage of gun and rod. It is a heritage of the open, which now must be idealized to a love of nature and a thoughtfulness of the meaning and preservation of life."

In that same year came an article by an avid hunter in the *Saturday Evening Post* celebrating conservation victories around the nation, and pushing for extended protection of elk south of Yellowstone, all in the name of sportsmanship. "This is an exceedingly good place and an exceedingly good time in the world's history to point out to all profiteering citizens that the Holdfast dog of American clean sportsmanship seems to be getting a habit of winning victories in the long run. Why not all act together and allow this victory to be won in the short run?" It's worth noting that during that part of the 19th century when hunting was allowed in Yellowstone National Park, it was hunters as much as any other group who led the charge to have the practice stopped.

All of which today can seem like some sort of distant golden age. Especially when presented with statements like those made recently by game warden John Hyde, who, when it comes to salting, wonders what all the fuss is about. "After all," Hyde remarked, "isn't baiting kind of like putting a worm on a hook?" Or assistant chief of the Wyoming Game and Fish Department's Wildlife Division, Harry Harju: "It may not be very cool to have salt sites strung along the boundaries of Yellowstone ... [but] if we can get another park elk killed that's probably a good thing."

THOUGH THE CHAOS IS RISING, LaVoy and I are nonetheless settling into a cheerful routine. Out of bed around 5:30 or 6:00 a.m.–depending on how late our visitors have stayed the night before and, at least for me, whether or not they were packing bourbon. Then a chilly plod to the outhouse, as often as not accompanied by the sound of a certain bear ripping apart logs on the hill behind the cabin. (The morning will soon come when, in the middle of taking care of business, LaVoy will have that same bruin amble within 10 or 15 yards of the outhouse, trapping him inside with the fingers of his good hand clutched around a can of pepper spray.) Each of us then writes for an hour or so before turning our attentions to pancakes or a bowl of five-grain cereal—mush, LaVoy calls it. Next a radio check-in with Judy at Blackrock Ranger Station, more writing, then out to clear trail or build fence, the latter task having turned into something close to an obsession to keep John Henry Lee's horses out of our pasture. In truth our fence building would earn few points for style. Armed with a couple dozen freshly made bucks, along with a few old rails scattered about in the willows and tall grass, we cobble the thing together into something that, even just constructed, looks instantly like a relic from the 19th century. But we push on with it, day after day, shoring up the most un-worthy sections with spikes and bailing wire, running out old pieces of electric fencing tape that will never be electrified, hop-ing John is right about his horses being trained to it, until at last the night comes when, by no small miracle, they no longer make it through.

A tall, wide ribbon of lupine continues to flower along the banks of the river, lending to every bend a lazy smear of blue the color of autumn sky. Fireweed is breaking open at the foot of Hawks Rest and in the old burns around Bridger Lake, toss-ing the land with millions of violet-colored blooms. Along the shore of the lake a pair of young bald eagles is in the nest, hanging tight and feasting on mom's fish dinners, even though the time has already passed when such birds typically fledge. Whenever I pass they're sitting stock-still in the nest staring into space, as if one has to first conjure a vision of flying before it's possible to actually do it. Meanwhile, young ravens are already off on their own, sitting in snags and soaring on the summer breezes, calling out about this and that in voices full of gravel and smoke.

With each passing week our fluency with the landscape grows a little stronger. These days we can anticipate the ebb and flow of things, from the honk of Canada geese on the Yellowstone to the drift of mule deer through the meadows at twilight. Having been several weeks in the backcountry, I find myself looking forward less to the sexy events—grizzly and wolf sightings, bolts of lightning stabbing the distant ridges—than to the simple, quiet seep of summer unfolding. There are more yampa blooms today than yesterday and fewer strawberries. The setting sun has inched southward from the notch at Lynx Creek to the high, stout walls of Two Ocean Plateau. The river sinks like a sigh, this week showing small rapids where days ago there was only a smooth skin of water. Were it not for my journal, I'd have absolutely no clue what day of the week it was. There's time enough to swim in the river and read in the sun; time enough to wait for thimbleberries to ripen and sandhill cranes to flush, for dawn to break and storms to pass. Of course, I still think about home now and then, but when I do it seems barely real.

At night we lay in our bunks like kids at camp, rambling the universe. I hear about the annual six-day survival trips LaVoy used to take his kids on beginning when they were eight or nine, dad and sons and daughters outfitted with nothing but a sleeping

bag and a hatchet. Most extraordinary of all, though, I hear one
night about how, after devoting nearly 40 years of his life to the
Mormon religion, LaVoy decided a decade ago the time had come
to examine every assumption he'd made about the faith. "All
along I'd been telling other people to take a hard look at their
lives. That if things didn't feel right, it might just be a sign the
time had come to do some personal searching. Now it was my
turn." Through hundreds of hours over the next three years he
wrote and read and reflected; in the end he felt he couldn't
escape the sense that the church was for him an artifice, stifling
what was most important about his own nature. "Once that
became clear it was pretty hard to carry on with things the way
they were." To the shock of absolutely everyone, he called a
meeting of the elders and asked to be excommunicated. If it was
a move that brought him a certain freedom, it also dumped in
his lap a divorce and a loss of friends; it even led one of his
neighbors to tack a note to the front door of his house calling
him a witch. "People would see me in the supermarket, or in the
post office," he recalls late one night, in the dark, "and rush off
in the other direction."

And so it happened that a man whose trajectory had been
largely set by a powerful, complex religion—one that in Utah has
the force of a freight train—would in the years that followed take
on a cosmology far less grandiose. At the core of his belief
today is a simple narrative he's told literally hundreds of times,
most often with kids in therapy: Jumping Mouse, arguably the
most famous Plains Indian tale of all time. A story about finding the courage needed to face doubt, betrayal, and paradox, all
in the service of trusting what instinctively feels like the right personal path. A tale about something inside incorruptible, about

the struggle a person sometimes has to go through in order to midwife his own reawakening. Nearly as useful to LaVoy—not to mention to a great many who've crossed paths with him—is the tale of Singing Stone, another layered story, common not only among the Plains Indians but in Celtic culture as well. Here a young boy is intrigued to learn from his grandmother of a magical stone lying somewhere in the land that offers the possessor unlimited wisdom and power. He devotes his life to finding it. After years of searching and exploring with various learned men, women, and even wizards—first in the north, then the south and west—he finally returns home to the east in late middle age only to find himself right back where he began. His mother, now old and quite frail, puts her arms around him and smiles. "Welcome home, Singing Stone," she says.

One particular night I'm up long after LaVoy falls asleep, awake when in the distance there begin flares of lightning and great claps of thunder. The storm is a big one, moving down the valley from the south, building in intensity until it's hovering right above our little cabin. The flashes come closer and closer together, finally topping one another, building to something like the finale of a fireworks show; on one occasion an explosion rings out like a rifle shot just beyond the front porch. Most remarkable of all are the sound effects added by the cliffs on either side of the valley, which serve as a kind of echo chamber. Multiple percussions roll up the Yellowstone as the storm drifts past northward, bouncing back and forth between the walls—complex, earth-shaking rhythms, by far the most dramatic spectacle since our arrival. The next morning the Yellowstone is up nearly a foot, muddy and sluggish. The air is scented with lupine and pine, the branches of the trees still dripping with rain.

Friends from home roll into this freshly washed world around midafternoon, and in the evening we circle up on the floor of the main room of the cabin–Kayla and several trail crew workers are there, too–while LaVoy teaches a class on making fires primitive fashion, using a wooden bow and drill. As usual he manages to turn what might sound like a camp trick into a kind of salon–questioning people about the meaning of fire, walking them through the cycle of carbon dioxide and water being turned into glucose by the sun, only to have the glucose released as carbon dioxide and water again through burning. All along the way he's pointing out big connections: the link between the vapor trail of a jet engine burning in the sky overhead, for example, and the vapor trails of our breath, made by trillions of tiny fires burning in our cells.

Later in the evening Kayla unfolds the current crop of mysteries she's struggling to unravel: the likely progression of the blister rust hopping across the drainages of the upper Yellowstone, the story behind a dead elk calf she found fully submerged and perfectly preserved in a still pool on the icy waters of Falcon Creek. She has a habit of ending her sentences by raising her voice inflection, which makes everything sound like a question–as if she's coaxing us along, checking to make sure we're still with her. Before heading back to camp she mentions having been on the north side of Rapid Creek earlier in the day, near its confluence with the Yellowstone, and coming across a black wolf maybe 150 yards away barking at her, running in a line parallel to her path, clearly agitated. There were tracks in the area, she says–lots of them, big and small. Figuring she was close to a den site she beat a hasty retreat. As the pups reach traveling age later this fall a routine will unfold, with the pack moving north toward the Yellowstone delta, west through the park toward Heart Lake, south to Fox Park, but then always home again to the Thorofare. Still doing that dance first established by Number 14 after leading her pack into this country five years ago. But for now, though, even though it's past denning season, the Delta pack seems content to stick close to home.

The following week I ask Bob Jackson for permission to camp on a hill inside Yellowstone Park, well above the Thorofare cabin, where we'll be able to put a spotting scope on the den site. Bob issues the permit, all right, but can't get through to dispatch in Mammoth so they can enter it into the main computer. Only after we've set up shop on the hill do I happen to remember that Laura Bush is in the area, touring the park, led by outfitter Gary Fales. While Secret Service planes are no doubt flying about looking for suspicious activity, here we are camped on a hill with a camouflaged spotting scope watching for wolves, hoping some blue suit doesn't see us and decide we're a couple of lunatics lying in wait for the President's wife. Over the course of our little stake-out, the mosquitoes are so bad we're forced to wrap ourselves in pile jackets and hats and balaclavas and gloves, and even then the little bastards have a field day feasting on the thin lines of flesh exposed along our wrists and upper cheeks.

The best news is that the afternoon is rich with sandhill cranes, gliding below us on six-foot wingspans with astonishing grace. Thanks in part to a windpipe that actually forms a loop within their breastbone, the call of these birds is a highly resonant chortle—a primal sound that seems firmly tethered to a dark and distant past. Indeed, sandhill crane fossils found in Nebraska have been aged at more than six million years old, making this the oldest still-living bird to be found anywhere on Earth.

Such is the bounty of elk passing in and out of the Thorofare during the warm months that this summer the Delta pack will set up only one rendezvous site, north of the den. Older brothers and sisters, aunts and uncles, and of course the alpha pair are even now taking on child care in shifts, staying near the pups not only to protect them from predators, but also to spend literally hours every day playing, wrestling, chasing each other's tails. (In years past I've even seen wolf packs engage in bouts of sledding on remnant snowfields.) Wolf behavior around the rendezvous site, as much as in any other season or location, is what many Native Americans are talking about when they explain how wolves served as models for interactions in their own cultures.

We're not back from our trek more than an hour before Jason and Jonathon, a pair of guides from Yellowstone Outfitters, drop in, eager to hear what we saw of the wolves. "That one pack," Jonathon says, referring to the Delta group, claiming his information is straight from the director of the wolf project, "it's up to 130 animals now." Not only that, he adds, but there are 485 wolves in the Thorofare alone. Clearly these are astonishing revelations. They mean the Delta pack is more than four times bigger than any wolf pack known to man, and if you extrapolate the Thorofare numbers to the rest of the ecosystem, in the past six months the wolf population has grown by a factor of 15, to some 3,000 animals. At that rate, I tell Jonathon, the food chain will be turned on its head, with predators outnumbering their prey.

"See what I mean, man?" he says. "We're in trouble here."

More and more Thorofare guides are showing up at the cabin these days, and every one of them is loaded not only with comments about wolves, but with double doses of the cowboy way. Many are skilled outdoorsmen—a proud and independent lot, quick to shake their heads in either sympathy or disgust over the unfortunate fates of the minions of corporate America. Yet in their own way they seem as bound to the herd as any group you could find. Not unlike the hip-hop culture of the inner city, this is a club based on talk, walk, and look. Central to the look is a .44 pistol in a holster on your hip, ideally with an empty bullet slot or two on the gun belt. Never mind that real cowboys almost never carried guns on their hips, as it was too easy to accidentally trip the trigger while holding the lead rope of a trailing horse. Finish off the outfit with scuffed chaps and riding boots—Vibram soles will get you laughed out of the wilderness—spurs, long sleeves, and a handkerchief around the neck; then take on a tobacco-stained Wyoming drawl just thick enough to cover up what for many is the great curse of having been born not in Wyoming but Ohio, New Jersey, or California. Whatever begrudging measure of respect is given to Forest Service, Park Service, or Game and Fish employees is based in large part on whether or not they look and act in similar fashion. "Most of these guys can't throw anything but a box hitch!" complains one of the most accomplished Forest Service packers on the district. "They're riding around in 90-degree heat wearing leather vests and kerchiefs, leading a bunch of dudes. What the hell have they got to be such badasses about?"

Be that as it may, nothing in this most remote place in the lower 48 is more astonishing than the degree to which things are run by outfitters and guides. A combination of bare budgets and weak will in the Forest Service has meant that enforcement of even the most basic regulations—those pertaining to illegal salting, only thing that works. In a sense the coming hunting season will seem to prove Fitzgerald right, as the outfitter he's been squaring off with for the past seven years will ride over to his camp and offer to bury the hatchet. "Still," he says, "I've seen this sort of thing wear down a lot of private hunters. Most guys just don't want to deal with the hassles."

Further undoing relations between privates and outfitters is a state law requiring a guide be on board for every two out-of-state hunters. Many resident sportsmen consider this outrageous, since it keeps them from having friends or even family members come in from other states to join them on their autumn hunts. It's exactly what state game warden Nate Wilson warned against in the 1918 State Game Warden's Report. Such a policy, argued Wilson, would cause the state to lose nonresident hunters' money—not just because of the extra expense of hunting with a guide, but from the fact that "it is very hard at times to get guides who make congenial companions, and if there is one thing a hunter despises, it is to have a disagreeable guide in camp."

Equally troubling is the strong perception by many that outfitters are given special favors. Packer policy from 50 years ago stated that "the number of horses will be limited to what is actually needed and used," a rule meant to discourage outfitters from bringing in enormous strings of stock animals for the chance to graze them on what even today is jokingly referred to as "that good government grass." Yet as time came to renew permits, some outfitters asked for and were given official permission to increase their animals. Whereas members of the general public coming into the Thorofare today are limited to 15 horses or mules, some outfitters are permitted five times that many. Barring that, there's always the trick of hiding extra horses and mules out of sight in nearby clefts and meadows, a maneuver I'll see employed more than once this summer.

"No permanent improvements will be allowed in the wilderness area," cautions a policy letter written long before the Wilderness Act, though cache platforms, oil drums, and even corrals continue to be fixtures of the forest. (It's true that in the 1970s it was decided that cache platforms could be used for food storage, part of an effort to reduce conflicts with grizzlies, but it was never intended that an outfitter would store food or gear outside his permitted use days the way many do today.) Official policy has also long promised that "after one warning, a dirty camp left by an outfitter shall be grounds for cancellation of campsite permit"—a threat that, despite obvious and numerous violations, has never been imposed. Former district ranger Don Hooper says he was outraged at what he saw as a double standard. "There've been times when whatever outfitters wanted the Forest Supervisor gave them." (Indeed, outfitters were so fond of his supervisor that they awarded him an honorary membership in the Wyoming Outfitters and Guides Association.) "Where natural resources are concerned, your land and my land, I don't think an outfitter or a rich or influential person should have any special privileges. But for a lot of my watch it was a matter of who you were and how much influence you had."

Early this summer an outfitter near Open Creek asked for special permission from Yellowstone rangers to travel to his camp through the Thorofare portion of the park, making his passage before the area technically opened for the season. The request was granted under the condition that he not overnight there. On his way out he discovered he couldn't make it in a single day, so was given emergency permission to spend the night in one of two sites. Not only didn't he stay where he was told, but in the grand tradition of condescension, took a crap right in the middle of the campsite without even bothering to dig a hole. Seasonal rangers issued a citation in absentia, but in the end their supervisor decided not to pursue it.

Clearly, if that part of the Wild West has been preserved in the Thorofare full of danger, requiring guides to be well seasoned, prepared for everything from blizzards to grizzlies, so too have we brought forward into this place a kind of cronyism that at times makes a mockery out of the democratic use of public lands.

CHAPTER SEVEN

*W*ITH THE CABIN REPAIRED AND THE FENCE
cobbled back together, firewood split and stacked for the
crews, LaVoy and I decide it's time to leave the wolf mania and
pasture wars, to load our packs and head for higher ground. It
takes us the better part of two days to reach the 11,000-foot mark
south of Blind Basin, the last several miles of which are spent
clamoring up a series of steep, trail-less ravines that no horseman
in his right mind would ever consider scaling. Hands and knees
hiking, climbing at a rate of more than 2,500 vertical feet per mile.
The views from the top are staggering. Narrow plates of tundra
spill out in all directions, split from each other by knife-edged
ridges and thousand-foot cliffs. Tight ravines tumble into lowlands thick with lupine and sticky geranium, currant and
Solomon's seal and bluebell. Even this high up, several massive
features loom still higher—Thunder Mountain, for one, looking
like summer quarters for Darth Vader. On the other side of
Thunder, on a nameless run of tundra, where almost no one ever

goes, is the wreckage of a light plane crash from some 40 years ago. There's an entry about it in the Hawks Rest logbook by a Forest Service ranger who came across it in the fall of 1993. "The people [from the plane] had been buried at the site and some of the bones were exposed and I covered them up and said a prayer. What a beautiful spot to be laid to rest."

It's here that the full impact of the Absaroka Range settles in, here that we can finally imagine the stunned alarm these peaks set off in early explorers—Hunt, Bonneville, and Raynolds to name but a few, the latter dumbfounded by Jim Bridger's warnings that his intended route north through these mountains from the Wind River Range would be impossible. But of all the predicaments such men found themselves in, perhaps that of Captain Bonneville's is the most telling. In all his thousands of miles of travel in the West, only here, south of where we now stand, was he utterly confounded. Lost and unable to make passage, the captain and a handful of men climbed for hours to reach a high promontory from which they hoped to figure a route west to the Green River. Standing astride the Continental Divide, wrote Washington Irving in *The Adventures of Captain Bonneville,* at that place the Indians regard as the crest of the world, gigantic peaks towering into the snowy reaches of the atmosphere,

> a scene burst upon the view of Captain Bonneville, that for a time astonished and overwhelmed him with its immensity.... Whichever way he turned his eye, it was confounded by the vastness and variety of objects. Beneath him, the Rocky Mountains seemed to open all their secret recesses: deep, solemn valleys; treasured

lakes; dreary passes; rugged defiles, and foaming torrents; while beyond their savage precincts, the eye was lost in an almost immeasurable landscape; stretching on every side into dim and hazy distance, like the expanse of a summer's sea. Whichever way he looked, he beheld vast plains glimmering with reflected sunshine; ... and snowy mountains, chain beyond chain, and peak beyond peak, till they melted like clouds into the horizon.... The captain stood for a long while gazing upon this scene, lost in a crowd of vague and indefinite ideas and sensations.

We know the feeling. Having gained a ridge at 11,400 feet, we look north to the sprawling backbone of Rampart Peak and, in the other direction, green tundra draped across the cone-shape flanks of Younts Peak. There are the tilted tablelands of Thorofare Plateau as well as the eroded cliffs of Blind Basin. But the vastness of the landscape is such that we can really only gather snapshots, a scene here and there—no chance whatsoever of grasping the whole, of understanding the exquisite entanglements of the range. "We've stumbled onto another continent," LaVoy murmurs.

The trance is broken by the sudden shiver of an oncoming storm, rolling in fast from the southwest. We start moving quickly to the south along a narrow knife edge of rock, in places 500 feet high and barely 3 feet wide, hoping to eventually cross the shoulder of a massive turret and begin the drop to the North Fork of the Yellowstone River. Thunder is booming now, lightning flashing several miles away, spearing the high ridges near

Younts Peak. Just when we think we might at least make the base of the turret, where we can probably crouch in a cranny and escape the worst of the weather, the knife edge we've been traversing comes to an abrupt end, dropping 40 feet straight down into a square notch blasted by the wind. We've got no choice but to retrace our steps, drop 500 feet into the rock-strewn valley to the east, and try to continue toward the Yellowstone from there. We make it off the spine just as hail begins pounding, scurry under the edges of a massive boulder where we wait and shiver, eat a little gorp and some jerky. Like everything else in the Absarokas the weather on any given day seems worthy of Greek myth. It never merely rains here. The sky bleeds the color of gun steel, and great tattered curtains of cloud meld and scatter before your eyes. The earth shakes under the boom of the thunder claps, and the growl of the reverberations bounce between the nearly vertical walls of surrounding canyons, drifting out mile after mile, one chorus barely fading before the next begins.

When the storm breaks we begin a slippery dance across a thousand yards of talus. In places the rocks are turned and rolled every which way—the handiwork of grizzlies, a number of them having been here not long ago in a search for cutworm moths. Fat little creatures, these moths, bellies the size of jelly-beans and full of protein, feeding at night on gardens of alpine wildflowers and then by day hiding in the crannies of these rocky slopes. Found at high elevations throughout the ecosystem, only here in the Absarokas are the cutworm moth's numbers sufficient to make grizzlies turn their backs on trout and berries and biscuit-root and run for the tundra. "There's one particular feeding site at an alpine cirque," says grizzly biologist Kerry Gunther, "where I've seen as many as nine and never fewer than five. We've got a grad student working there now, and she's watched a dozen bears, all feeding within a couple hundred yards of each other."

Much to the aggravation of farmers, cutworm moths lay their eggs in commercial fields in lowland valleys. Once pupated they migrate to the high country to feed on the nectar of blooming tundra plants, returning to the low country to lay their eggs the following fall. This is not a new item at the grizzly café. Bear researchers in the 1940s write about having trouble luring grizzlies into their baits, simply because they were up here stuffing themselves with moths. This summer a researcher studying the melting of glaciers in the Wind River Range will bring Kerry Gunther a bag of debris found in the prehistoric ice; in it will be moth parts, layer after layer, hundreds and even thousands of years old.

This habit grizzlies have of making meals out of tiny creatures, from ants to grubs to worms, has long seemed at odds with the popular fantasy of big bears eating in big bites. "It is a little remarkable," wrote traveler Colvin Verplanck about the grizzly in 1872, "that even the great savage of our continent grows less and dwindles in our estimation as we near his home. What have we to say when we learn that this mighty beast, at certain seasons of the year, devotes the whole of his majestic mind and body to the capturing and eating of grasshoppers?" Of course there's time enough for bigger fare, from elk calves in the spring and then spawning cutthroat trout. With fall comes the elk rut, and in active places like Hayden Valley several bulls will be gored and bears will get them as well. When wolves make kills the bears are often close behind, sometimes running the pack off and claiming the meat for themselves. Two years ago, biologists watched as wolves began to kill a young bison, only to have a grizzly come along and finish the job. On another occasion, near Mount Everts, an elk scrambling out onto the ice to escape pursuit by wolves broke through; once again a grizzly blustered in, killing the animal in the water and dragging it to shore. Even so, a great share of the calories ingested by the mighty bear come from plants and grubs and grasshoppers and moths.

An hour more of hiking and we finally gain a ridgeline high above the North Fork of the Yellowstone. The only problem is that although the ravines leading to the valley floor begin at a modest grade, once over the lip of the tundra they plunge in near vertical fashion, making free-falls of 60 to 100 feet. We try one and then another until, after much wandering about and scratching of heads, we find a drop that looks doable. Even here the trek is rugged, made more so by an absence of any plant life to secure the soil; instead there are handfuls of dirt and loose scree the size of marbles, making for uncertain footing at every step. Even the big rocks—the ones the size of washing machines and refrigerators—which in other parts of the Rockies you could count on for solid footing, seem ready to tumble with the lightest step. One way or another this range seems determined to shake us, be it with grizzlies or crumbling rocks or sheer cliffs or weather strong enough to blow us off the tundra. By the time we stagger into camp I'm thinking people should visit places like this only now and then. Should come here trembling, clutching in their frozen fingers sacrifices and charms.

We've called it quits some 800 feet above the North Fork of the Yellowstone, on what seems the only flat patch of ground anywhere in sight. Maybe it's the lightning storm or that knuckle-biting slip-'n'-slide off the tundra, but LaVoy is once again full of great thoughts. Over a pot of soup he announces he's decided to have his remains cremated and scattered in the desert of southern Utah. Of course, he'll have to share this decision with his kids at the end of summer, he explains, which leaves me wondering if it was a choice made right here in the backcountry, in the rarefied air of the upper Absarokas. It's the right thing to do, he says, in accord with absolutely everything going on around us. He flicks a finger toward a large Englemann spruce beside the tent. "That tree right there. Think how it starts out, growing really fast. Then it reaches its potential, gets as big and strong as it can be given the environment it lives in. And one day it begins to decay. It's an old tree, leaning a bit, showing the wear and tear of life. A few limbs might hang on, still showing some greenery, but eventually it runs out of energy. Falls over and dies."

LaVoy is a fan of the pregnant pause, often leaving enough space in his comments to drive a truck through. "So there's some kind of reassurance in that?" I ask. "Does it leave you any more comfortable with your own death?"

He grins under a full beard, smiling and as calm as if we were trading jerky recipes. "It's more than that," he says. "I hate this whole idea we have of trying to delay, even prevent decay—part of the process I call life. Put people in lead-lined caskets because we can't stand the unavoidable. But it's like that tree. You die and you turn into something inanimate. Then pretty soon you're flying on the wings of the animate again." He's wound up now, grinning and waving his hands. Most of a decaying body gets turned into carbon dioxide and oxygen, he says, some of which probably flies halfway around the world as molecules of water. "The carbon dioxide might get taken up by that little flower there by your foot. And with a little photosynthesis it's turned into sugar, and that sugar gets eaten by a bear. That's immortality, brother!

"Maybe you can't hear all the people and organisms speaking to you in the living world, but they're here. They're definitely here." It's as though I've slipped through a time warp and ended up spooning soup with John Muir. "The destruction was in fact creation," Muir wrote about the obliteration of forests by volcanoes north of here, on Yellowstone's Specimen Ridge. "Progress in the march of beauty through death." Admittedly, the basis of this slice of LaVoy's cosmology is a bit less eloquent—something he likes to call the Alka-Seltzer theory. "Think of the water in the glass as the universe. Then think of yourself as an Alka-Seltzer, expanding over time through endless cycles of life and death to become a part of the whole. Rising up to contribute to it, become a part of it."

All in all these epiphanies seem to have left him more certain than ever of his choices. "I'm an ornery little bastard," he says. "I know I am. But right now I'm casting off the shackles. It's like when I was born I was the nucleus of the onion. But over time I've had so much put on me by the culture, by the expectations of family and friends. I've always been resistant of that because it corrals me. It's nothing more than a form of domestication."

We put some water on to boil for hot chocolate, watch as the clouds break in the west to let in the sun. "I'm telling you," LaVoy says quietly. "If there's an afterlife better than this, I don't think I could stand it."

All the while we're up here imagining ourselves circling the globe in microscopic form, unbeknown to us Kayla is just a few miles to the south, having a peak insight of her own. We hear about it back at Hawks Rest, when she sits in the director's chair and takes a couple of deep breaths through her nose, checking her emotions. The woman who when it comes to grizzlies has had more dances than a hurdy-gurdy girl, has on this day experienced the closest bear encounter of her life. It was in the morning, she tells us, well off any trail, out of the wind on the north side of a patch of forest. "I was about done packing up camp, was reaching into my pack to grab the sunscreen." She pauses for a long minute, takes another breath. "I turned around and there was a sow grizzly and two cubs not 35 feet away, walking right toward me. I've seen a lot of bears. But this was the only time I ever saw my life flash in front of my eyes." She says she let out a scream—an involuntary one—at which point the bear stopped, began to slowly turn. Having seen the success of that outburst she issued another one, just as loud. And with that the bear family simply ambled away.

When Kayla first came to the wilderness she was deeply involved in the Pentecostal Church. "I'd go out on my trips in the wilderness and see things going one way, then I'd go to town, to church, and everything seemed to be heading in the opposite direction. For me it was the wilderness that proved to be the most real." Still, I'm thinking there must be nothing like a dicey grizzly encounter to rekindle the heart of a fundamentalist. (As one writer put it, the grizzly is an Old Testament god.) Maybe it's some shred of that old faith wrapped in new clothing that allows Kayla to carry pepper spray but never come close to using it. Needless to say, she wouldn't even consider hauling a gun around, a choice that seems to rankle some of the macho, gun-toting cowboys (who should of course be eternally grateful the big bear is here in the first place, since without it they'd look completely silly). "She's a liar," John Henry Lee tells LaVoy matter-of-factly, discounting Kayla's escapades as pure fiction.

🍂

CAVAN FITZSIMMONS SITS AT THE TABLE at Hawks Rest—a smudged felt hat cocked over his boyish face, a cheap fork in one hand and a pocketknife in the other—waiting to eat a steak cooked just past bloody off a plastic plate. A former football player, he has the roguish good looks of a movie star with none of the effort. Sitting next to him is his partner on this shift, Jason, a thin, wiry man even more covered in soot than most, whose size belies his ability both to eat like a bear as well as to spend hour after hour fast dancing with a crosscut saw. "Had everything today but an encounter with an endangered species," Cavan says, recounting a wreck two hours earlier when a cross-cut saw came off one of the mules, as well as the usual trail work, policing dirty camps, catching people building fires despite the fire ban. "Yeah, I knew there was a ban," one guy told him at Two Ocean Pass. "But I didn't think there was much chance of running into you."

Testosterone runs thick in the Thorofare, and one of the ways it shows up in trail crews is through an obsession to do more work than anyone else in a given day. Cavan isn't just a worka-holic, some say, but a work maniac. And while that may fit well with Jason, who can match him step for step, other people Cavan has worked with this summer have been muttering under their breath that he's one crazy bastard. Several years ago, when it was just Cavan working the entire northern end of the Teton Wilderness, he'd routinely ride 250 miles on every shift, trying hard to show as much presence as possible to outfitters. Three weeks from now his girlfriend, Sally, will come on board as a volunteer for an eight-day hitch—a chance, she figures, to see what her beau does for a living—and she too will nearly be run into the ground.

Perhaps in part because of their age, many of these seasonals still have in their pockets some fine shavings of idealism. The son of a horse trainer and a federal judge, Cavan truly believes he's making a difference here. "My mom was great," he tells me over a cocktail of vodka and Gatorade, trying to explain the origins of his can-do attitude. "When I was about 11 years old, I wanted a horse. But instead of just giving me one she gave me a broodmare, told me to find a stud horse and breed her, so that's what I did. She knew I'd have to care for that mare during her pregnancy, then raise the colt. Only after all that, once I had a relationship with it, would I be able to ride. By the end I understood something about the investment it takes to get what you want."

I offer to cook up the steaks and vegetables the boys brought in so they can kick back and relax, and once again the talk goes on until midnight. Idealism aside, Cavan does seems to struggle now and then—at least in the late hours, when the need for sleep is pulling on him—trying to reconcile what needs to be done on this forest with his limitations as a seasonal. The fresh order that just came down prohibiting hunting within 200 yards of a salted site—that one he knows to be more or less unenforceable, at least until the salts are clearly marked, and few people on the forest even know where they are. Besides, as LaVoy points out, if the law is meant to keep outfitters from hunting over existing salts, what's there to prevent them from simply creating new ones? No one even bothers to mention the most obvious problem, which is how less than a handful of people are going to patrol 300 square miles of land, showing up at the right moment to catch someone shooting in the wrong place.

If Cavan continues to make it in this free-for-all, it'll be in part because of his sense of humor. Over a dessert of cookies and M&M's, he recalls the time last year when he rode up on someone with his tent set up right next to a stream. Told that he'd have to move a hundred feet from the water, the guy unclipped his holster, turned his pistol around, leaned forward and growled: "Fuck you, pine pig." Cavan says the pine pig part cracked him up, that he laughed so hard that in the end the guy ended up laughing about it too; before long the two of them were moving the tent. When he first started working here he was told by other rangers to "disbelieve pretty much everything you hear, unless you have clear proof it's true"—a piece of advice he now passes on to newcomers. With outfitters it's a game, he explains, always a game.

Last week he stumbled across a camp and found a huge fire burning, right in the middle of the fire ban. The outfitter tried to explain it away, saying one of his clients had fallen in the creek and they were just trying to warm him. "It was bullshit, of course," Cavan says, no particular rancor in his voice. "But you have to pick your battles. Instead of asking the outfitter what the guy was wearing, where on the creek it happened, then asking the same questions to the guide, I let it go. You can piss people off by riding them too hard." The approach couldn't be more different than Bob Jackson's. Indeed, Cavan says Bob's a great help to him in a good cop/bad cop kind of way. "All I have to say to some outfitter is 'well, I'm not going to be a Bob Jackson with you on this,' and right away things turn." Still, he says he gives everyone a single "get-out-of-jail-free card," and then the next time it's a citation.

It's worth noting that like a lot of other Forest Service rangers—even, believe it or not, like Bob Jackson—neither Jason nor Cavan think more law enforcement is the answer to every problem on the Teton Wilderness. They may be happy to write tickets for salting, for example, but feel the real change will come only through hunters becoming educated—that in the end clients will do what the agencies won't. Cavan talks about the remarkable improvement in compliance with no-trace camping practices among outfitters, which he credits mostly to education. "It took 15 years," he says, "but back here 15 years is nothing."

The trail crews in a given wilderness are so valuable because they're among the few people in the Forest Service who spend time on the ground. Although even the best supervisors, including Teton Wilderness manager Rob St. John, may want desperately to get out on the trail, they do so only with great difficulty, largely because they're buried under mountains of paperwork. For them as well as for the public, workers like Cavan and Jason, Dustin, Lori, and Darren and Kate are a godsend, willing to pull monster shifts for crappy pay for no other reason than that they love being out here. Of course, some full-timers could care less who's out here in the woods, treating a district-level job as nothing more than a stepping-stone to the supervisor's office— or, better yet, regional headquarters. They're the dangerous ones, everyone tells me, prone to slashing budgets just to prove how much of a tightwad they can be, all the while letting the resource go to hell. Sadly, these are also the people who often make it to the top. Which, of course, means they're the ones making key decisions about what, if anything, becomes a priority issue on national forestland.

Such indifference is a far cry from the guys who first wore the big hats around here. Ranger Rudolph "Rosie" Rosencrans for one, the man who patrolled this country through much of the first half of the 20th century. Born the son of a forester in a small village in Austria, Rosie knew even as a young boy that he was bound to cross the big water and ride into that exotic land called Wyoming—a spark lit on a family holiday in Vienna, when the Rosencrans family happened to catch Buffalo Bill Cody's Wild West show. The short of it is that Rosie was one of those kids who couldn't wipe the dreams off his shoes. When it came time to sign up for his obligatory hitch in the military he chose the navy, figuring it would afford him the best chance of landing in America. And so it happened that when his ship the *Princess Elizabeth* finally put into port in San Francisco, having made calls from China to the South Seas, Rosie left the sailor's life and headed, at last, to the Rocky Mountains.

Rosie Rosencrans, much like Cavan and company, could work like a mule. One year while he was employed at a ranch along Wyoming's Green River, a blizzard marooned a large herd of cattle. Figuring the only chance to save them was to round up help and build a trail to the animals, Rosie strapped on his skis and headed out to gather neighbors, schussing through a blizzard for 27 hours straight, covering a whopping 82 miles. Done with that he headed right back in to the herd, meeting up with the other men he'd rounded up, wielding a shovel for hours in a desperate, though ultimately successful attempt to dig them out. Far worse than the actual work, he'd recall later, was the fact that the woman who owned the ranch never even bothered to say thanks.

From the start this was a man driven by strong notions of justice. When on his first trip to Jackson he learned his traveling partner was planning to hole up there and become a counterfeiter, a fight broke out and Rosie nearly got his head cracked with a .45; thanks to some strong talk and fast fists, though, the man finally agreed to head back where he came from and leave the town of Jackson alone. Rosie began his life as a forest ranger in 1904, signing on for the grand sum of $60 a month, two good horses, and all the necessary equipment. For much of his career it wasn't counterfeiters but poachers that pushed his buttons, sending him down the trail to chase some of the baddest bad guys in the West.

In the early 20th century one of the region's most notorious poaching bands was the Binkley-Purdy-Isabel gang—a clever, if motley crew of locals who routinely moved through Yellowstone killing elk for racks, hides, and front teeth (so-called "tusks"), which they then sold for high dollars throughout the West. Knowing full well the risk of being caught by Army scouts, who by that time were making regular patrols of the park's backcountry by hopping between snowshoe cabins, the gang preferred to do their poaching in bad weather using small caliber rifles—ones that when fired would produce a noise that carried no more than a hundred yards. (At one point Ed Binkley and the boys took that concept a step further still, fashioning crude silencers.) If it were the teeth they were after, once an elk was down the men might leave it for several days, thereby minimizing their exposure to patrols. What's more, when retrieving animal parts they often traveled with boards strapped to their boots to which they'd fastened elk feet, all in an effort to disguise their tracks. In one of their better ruses Binkley showed up one day in Judge Pierce Cunningham's chambers claiming to have run into a notorious poacher everyone was looking for. While the posse was hot on that tip, Binkley and gang were elsewhere, gathering up great heaps of wildlife booty and then making a beeline for Idaho, where they were poised to ship some $10,000 worth of hides and teeth to Los Angeles. Alas, it wasn't their day. A small dog running loose was drawn to the smell of the burlap bags; he tore one open and revealed the contents to shipping authorities.

It was due to some remarkable sleuthing by Rosie over several weeks that the federal government was finally able to link those poached hides and teeth to Yellowstone Park. Unlike the incident with the marooned cattle, when the ranch owner offered not a shred of thanks for Rosie's heroic efforts, this time there was gratitude aplenty. "No more efficient ranger ever threw a diamond hitch," gushed the semi-weekly *Pocatello Tribune*, "and a handier man on webs or skis never buckled to a long slope of gleaming snow. Stockily built, with legs like Hercules, clad in khakis, wide of shoulder, deep of chest … such is the man who tracked Purdy and Binkley." Other writers would characterize him as "blood brother of the grizzlies," the kind of guy who walks around "with eyes wide open as men's are who fear nothing."

One of the biggest disputes Rosie had with locals was over how ranchers were using salt for their cattle on national forestlands. Despite instructions from managers to place their salt blocks evenly across the range, thereby achieving a more equal use of the available graze, cattlemen were set on merely dumping them out along streams, as they'd been doing for decades. Rosie tried time and again to explain to ranchers that their animals would fare better under the new system, but he might as well have been talking to tree stumps. Exasperated, he finally gathered up the salt blocks, packed them onto horses, and carried them to other locations. "They found out it worked," he said years later. "That cured them." When he wasn't cajoling ranchers or nabbing poachers Rosie was digging fire lines, building cabins and even a ranger station, and, in one case, escorting a frightened elderly doctor across a swollen river with a rope tied around him, leading him to the cabin of a woman in the throes of childbirth.

One day in 1913, while out riding the ridgeline above Thorofare Creek, Rosie spotted a large party of men on the stream bank below; he decided to head down and swap greetings. To his astonishment, standing at the center of the group was an older, distinguished-looking fellow with white hair. There was no mistaking his childhood hero, Buffalo Bill Cody. Cody and his guides had been searching with no luck for a place called Blind Basin; fortunately for them Rosie knew every nook and cranny of that country, and he was only too happy to show the way. "Never have I enjoyed a trip more," Buffalo Bill said later. So thrilled was he, in fact, so grateful was he to his newfound guide that, on returning to camp, he offered Rosie a souvenir of anything he saw. To everyone's amazement the forest ranger asked for a lock of Cody's hair. It was a request that surprised even the old showman, causing him to step away for a few minutes to give the matter some serious thought. Finally Cody reached back into the thickest part of his locks, gathered a few strands and offered them to Rosie, who drew his knife and carefully cut them from his head.

Local historians say that a combination of writing journals and making detailed maps, often in poor light, along with several bad bouts of snow blindness, caused severe damage to Rosie's vision. The condition grew so bad that in his late 50s he was forced to leave the Forest Service, even though he was otherwise still strong as a mule. The old ranger would live another 42 years, eventually going completely blind, residing in a small, tree-shrouded cabin on a side street in downtown Jackson.

CHAPTER EIGHT

*T*RAIL CREWS HAVE LEFT; THE COWBOY GUIDES have returned. Today it's Bob who's folded into the cabin's old director's chair, a laconic, "shucks-ma'am" guy of about 25. Over a cup of coffee he tells about being out last night about 10:30 under a full moon, having just rounded up some horses that had skedaddled to a distant pasture near Senecio Creek, when a big grizzly stood up in the trail and sent the whole string bolting in the other direction. As for Bob, he ended up holding on for dear life, trying like crazy to stay out of the rope. "I called that bear everything but a white man," he says, shaking his head. "But he just looked at me, finally took off runnin'."

Fish are down and elk are up, Bob tells us, says he's looking forward to another good hunting season. It's a far different picture than the one being painted up north, in the Gallatin National Forest, for years considered one of the best elk hunting locations in the country—second only to this one. Indeed, out of all elk killed in the state of Montana, a whopping 55 percent are taken in hunting districts bordering Yellowstone. Outfitters on the Gallatin who used to brag about 80 percent kill rates, though, are as of late seeing numbers only half that good. Of course many blame the devil wolf, and in truth wolves play a small part. The northern range supports tremendous year-round elk populations, and those, in turn, support great numbers of the predators who feed on them—not just wolves, but mountain lions and coyotes, black bears and grizzlies. "On a per pack basis," says wolf biologist Doug Smith, "all wolves have about the same kill rate. But the density is a lot higher up here than it is down in the Thorofare."

Some researchers feel that elk may be near carrying capacity on the northern range, which would bring into play a common population limiting device—a so-called "density dependence factor." This dynamic has to do with the fact that as elk populations become dense cows are likely both to carry less fat and produce fewer calves; what young are born tend to have lower birth rates, which means fewer of them survive. Furthermore, these animals have spent the past four years dealing with serious drought, a condition long known to affect the health of wildlife in general. Such explanations seem more plausible than wolves, especially when you consider that the number of calves born into the herds—a number referred to as the recruitment rate—has also been down in parts of Montana where wolves aren't present. Finally, it's worth noting that hunter participation on the northern range is also down. Some of that might be due to the fact that most of the trees burned in the 1988 fires have now toppled, resulting in fewer people being willing to go off trail to pursue their quarry. That, and the fact that some sportsmen seem increasingly reluctant to hunt in places where they might have to argue with grizzlies over their kills.

Soon after cowboy Bob saddles up and rides away the other, more famous Bob returns—ranger Bob Jackson from Yellowstone. He asks if I'd like to help search out some illegal salting sites, some of which were located last summer by University of Montana graduate student Dustin Walters as part of a master's thesis on revegetation. In truth I've been wanting to follow up on some of Walters' work, especially after stumbling across a telling entry he made in the Hawks Rest logbook. "I walked into this salting thinking I was simply working on a graduate thesis research project," he wrote in August 2000. "After talking to folks in the back country I realize I've stepped into a rather large political issue. Just praying that I don't get shot by outfitters in September."

We decide to leave the next morning, traveling cross-country on foot up the steep back side of Hawks Rest, where we'll comb for sites along a high ridge above Thorofare Creek. We're barely two miles out before a nasty storm blows in from the west, hammering us with truckloads of marble-size hail. As the whole area is severely burned we find little protection; finally crawl under a small cluster of lodgepole to wait it out, eat a little, try to have a conversation, but the ice makes so much noise drumming against our hoods and the bills of our caps that about all we can do is scream at one another. The ice knocks the blooms off the aster and the fireweed and rolls into the washes—in a matter of 20 minutes gathers there two inches deep. When it finally quiets a bit Bob launches into some good tales, including one about sitting utterly still in the woods at night on a stakeout for poachers, only to have a big grizzly come along and look him right in the face.

Bob explains that he had his mind set on a life in the boondocks long before he ever set foot in Yellowstone, having as a
kid been drawn to anything and everything having to do with
the outdoors. His classmates back in Iowa were so struck by the
strong bent both he and his older brother Bill showed for hunting, fishing, and running trap lines (the latter which they managed
at 5:30 every morning, on their way to school), they were soon
nicknamed "the great white hunters"—a moniker duly noted in
the high school yearbook. In the end all three Jackson boys went
on to get degrees in fish and wildlife biology from Iowa State;
following graduation Bob took the required tests for a job with
the government, scored high, and ended up in Yellowstone—first
as a seasonal working for the Bureau of Sport Fisheries, then later
as a Park Service fire guard on the Lake District.

Getting a ranger slot in Yellowstone has been difficult for
a very long time, but rarely more so than in the early to mid-
1970s. In part this was due to enormous interest by baby boomers
in environmental jobs, but also because at the time there was a
wash of veterans flooding the government job market; like
today, veterans were given strong hiring preferences. Still, Bob's
supervisors on the Lake District were awfully impressed with this
Iowa farm boy—his initiative, how he handled horses, the way
he could work without supervision. So in a move that given Bob's
current troubles seems a bit ironic, then-Superintendent Jack
Anderson took the unusual step of claiming one of the five sec-
retarial appointments to Yellowstone that senators and other big
players are typically handed each year, spending it to land Bob
Jackson in a backcountry ranger position.

When the storm finally passes it leaves plenty of cold in
its wake. Temperatures are hovering somewhere in the low 40s,

and during the entire climb up the back of Hawks Rest we're trudging on hailstones congealed into layers of slush. Between slips and slides the conversation comes back to the usual focal point—one bizarre tale after another of some outfitter gone bad. In truth Bob has caught a fair number of guides poaching over the years, and, once or twice, outfitters themselves. He's a part of the reason why it's illegal to carry even dismantled guns into the park, as well as the spark behind a rule change that no longer allows hunters to follow wounded game into Yellowstone. "I actually found guys with bloody snowballs in their pockets," he explains, "squeezing out blood trails as they walked. That way they could say they shot an elk outside the park and it ran across the border—there was the blood sign in the snow to prove it." At one point I make the comment that some of their shenanigans sound pretty clever, but Bob will have none of that. "Bullshit!" he says. "These guys are breaking the law. When I catch somebody poaching there's none of this shaking hands crap, acknowledging them as a worthy opponent. The simple fact is I'm right and they're wrong." Bob Jackson is obsessed with poachers, happy to track them for hours, for days, as often as not on foot, in snow and sleet and hail. "I need to know everything about these guys. I think of them all the time when I'm on the horse. You have to consider everything— what they were reading in *Outdoor Life* as little kids, the romance they bring from all that into the hunting season." (Bob himself remembers swooning over ads in that magazine enticing readers to "hunt, trap and fish" as a government trapper.) He says that when he finally catches poachers, almost without exception they break down. "They're sitting there in tears—all of them except Nate, anyway. I quietly hand them a pad of paper and a pen, they write their confession and sign it, and it's all over."

The sky breaks open as we near the top of the saddle, and with the change of weather comes a change in stories. Bob's telling now about how he's seen even rangers and wardens "go native" out here, tossing their hat in with the outfitters because good, bad, or otherwise they're the ones who call the shots on this forest. "Order seeks disorder," he says, recapping his water bottle after a mighty swig. "Truth is it feels good to sit around the fire with the boys, have a drink, and chew the fat. Be offered dinner and a cup of coffee on a cold night. Get your horse shod, go back to the cabin and read Louis L'Amour." If he's right about people seeking order, it's hard not to wonder about the long-term effect of his having been thoroughly cut loose—hated by most outfitters, and at the same time working without any meaningful support from the Park Service. There's little doubt he still has the bit in his teeth (the buzz in the front country among Park Service employees is that with Senators Baucus and Grassley in his corner, he's untouchable), but every now and then I sense he's not getting the satisfaction out of all this that he once did. At the point the Park Service ditched him, he confesses, "right then it stopped being fun."

Whatever order there is out here for Bob is based to no small degree on what found purchase in his head years ago, right along with his fierce passion for the outdoors. A vision of good guys and bad guys and right and wrong behavior woven together not just from decades years in the backcountry, but from choices made in the green fields of Iowa. The Jackson kids endured a certain amount of mocking for what might be called their hand-me-down look—the result not of poverty, but the fact that Bob's father was more interested in spending his modest earnings as a farmer on college for his five kids than on school fashions. Beyond that there was no shortage of bullies making life miserable for his dyslexic sister as well as for a brother with a cleft palate—and Bob was always more than happy to take them on. "It wasn't fair," he says, "and I wouldn't stand for it." Years later, he found it easy to transfer his urge to protect onto the animals of Yellowstone. "It's all just part of the circle of life," he's told me. "And the more you're in the backcountry the more you realize you're just a part of it, a piece of this larger whole." It's worth noting that Jackson often describes the salting issue in a way that frames everyone involved in terms of a basic lack of respect—not just for the grizzly and the elk, but for clients who think they're getting a wild hunt, when in fact it's little more than "game farm hunting without fences." Even the guides are getting ripped off, he says, first when a boss asks them to break the law by placing salt, and again every time they help finagle the deception.

Whether you think Bob is on a heroic crusade—something akin to the Lone Ranger, as *Los Angeles Times* writer Frank Clifford suggested—or whether, as his supervisor had the lack of good sense to tell a journalist from Missoula, he's "certifiable," he's without question driven by a clean set of principles. (One fellow this fall, thinking out loud on the Internet in a Yellowstone chat room, pondered whether Bob might in fact be in cahoots with the poachers. Rest assured he'd sooner impale himself on a stake.) And yet those principals are being carried by a man increasingly alone in a lonely place, wrapped in the kind of solitude that in time can make it hard to tell the difference between real bullies and mere phantoms. "I have to keep this all in perspective," he told me once. "I have to understand why I'm doing this, what my mental state is. Without it you just become a product of your environment."

Bob's case against the outfitters isn't helped by the fact that he sometimes has a hard time turning his back on a good story. It's no doubt true, for example, that some outfitters have killed grizzlies illegally, may well be doing so today. But on several occasions he's told LaVoy and me about burial grounds, "grizzly graveyards" scattered about the wilderness. On a trek two weeks ago LaVoy and I even stopped to look for one, supposedly located behind a certain outfitter's camp, but in the end found not a shred of evidence. And besides, if bears really are buried around the Teton Wilderness, why not just go and dig them up? In short, if Bob hears something dicey about an outfitter he's going to believe it, no less than the outfitters believe every lousy thing they hear about him. Maybe it's just proof that anyone who spends much time in the backcountry will—in the grand tradition of Jim Bridger—sooner or later turn into a purveyor of tall tales.

The depth of Bob's disdain for the outfitting industry, at least as it's played in the Thorofare, was underscored one rainy afternoon when his partner, Frank Deluka, stopped by our cabin—a compact, broad-shouldered guy of 33 whom we first met on the northeast corner of Yellowstone Lake, at the Ninemile Trailhead. Frank's a man on the lower rungs of the Park Service ladder but on his way up, slowly, almost casually, the way a person might saunter to the corner store for a loaf of bread when he knows no one's back home waiting for it. A former firefighter from New Jersey, he tosses off an easy smile, yet always has an eyebrow raised, a good guy who's willing to listen to anybody's story, but aware that half of what he hears is probably bullshit.

For that matter, Frank himself isn't above slinging a bit of it now and then. Like when he tells outfitters he's not from New Jersey but Pinedale, Wyoming—the town he worked out of for a short time as a seasonal backcountry ranger. The fib, he explains, is intended to better his chances of not being blown off. As for the New Jersey accent, that, he tells them, comes from having gone to school there. Frank says a lot of outfitters have spent their entire lives riding this country and they aren't especially fond of some guy from the East Coast who knows next to nothing about horses trying to tell them how to run their business. As a case in point he tells of a ranger in his 20s at Tower this summer, long hair and wire-rim glasses, can barely ride a horse—"the kid looks less like a ranger than somebody you'd meet at a rave club." The kid comes up to an outfitter and tells him he should spray more Fly-Swipe on his horses so they won't roll in the dirt so much and damage the resource. Which sort of misses the fact that with or without insect repellent horses and mules just plain like to roll in the dirt. At any rate, kid ranger is halfway through telling this outfitter he's going to be a good guy, won't cite him for the infraction, when the outfitter goes nuts, screams at the kid to get the hell out of his camp and never show his face again. The outfitter was still fuming days later when he called the district ranger, demanding the kid be fired. "It makes them crazy," Frank says. "Somebody from Wyoming, though, sometimes they'll cut 'em a little slack."

When Frank left the Forest Service this year to take a seasonal law enforcement position in Yellowstone, little did he know he'd end up spending most of the summer in the Thorofare, as often as not under the tutelage of none other than Bob Jackson. In some ways the two couldn't be more different. Frank with his easy-going attitude, unwilling to write anything more severe than a warning, and Bob with his take-no-prisoners attitude. "I don't think Bob's ever met an outfitter he likes," Frank observes. "He'll ride seven miles out of his way just to visit one of their camps. We're supposed to do a performance evaluation on these guys once a year; Bob does one every time he sees them."

Bob, meanwhile, says being aggressive is the only way to handle these guys. "You've gotta understand what we're dealing with here," he tells me on the trail today. "One day I'm out patrolling on foot when Randy Haecker comes down the trail. Kicks his horse and runs right for me. But I don't budge. Comes so close I could've yanked him off the saddle. 'One of these days somebody's going to shoot you, Jackson!' he shouts." To which Bob offers an instant reply: "Well, they'd better get me with the first shot!" There've been other threats, other wrongs. Twice people have tried to poison his horses—succeeding on one occasion, though it wasn't fatal. Another time somebody came in at night and scattered porcupine quills across a wallow used by his mules. "It's like when you're playing football or any of the sports," Bob says. "You've gotta elevate the energy level, be able to put it out." He freely admits that the one problem with that approach is that it goes completely against government protocol, which demands you do everything you can to get along. "But they don't understand what's going on back here. You'll never gain the respect of these outfitters because they see themselves as being on the opposite side. Their agenda is a lot different than mine. I don't like to be in confrontational situations, but that's what it takes to survive."

Frank Deluka actually defends Bob far more than he crit-
icizes him, gives him credit for having enormous knowledge and
experience. He thinks it's a shame people in the park have been
so quick to turn their backs on him. "I've had guys in the front
country call Bob a liar for saying he's been around the
Thorofare for almost 30 years. But last week I was reading
the old logbooks, thought I'd see what was going on back in
1969, the year I was born. Sure enough, there was an entry
telling how Bob and this other ranger were out on patrol,
looking for poachers." Others in the park, Frank says, some in
fairly prominent positions, discount Bob's efforts to nab poachers, saying there's been little in the way of poaching in the
Thorofare in modern times. Again, he says, the logbooks tell
a different story. "I don't know," Frank concludes. "I'm like most
firefighters, into tradition. They come in and want to build you
a new station, as a firefighter you fight like hell against that.
You wanna keep the place you're in—the brick building from
1940 with the gargoyles on the roof. A lot of the guys at
Yellowstone don't seem to care much for tradition. What happened in the past doesn't matter. It's only what's happening
under their watch that counts. Bob's done a lot for the tradition of this place. And now no one wants to touch him."

By early afternoon Bob and I are standing on a high ridge
some thousand feet above Thorofare Creek, looking at the near
flank of The Trident, which forms the southern boundary of
Yellowstone. Every drainage, every feature prompts a story.
"See that high cliff above the ravine?" Bob asks, raising his arm
and pointing directly across the valley. "That's Aspen Creek,
where I caught two guys gut-shooting an elk—shot at it 14 times
from a good half mile away. Now go two drainages over. That's

Cat Creek; it's been called that since I caught Nate Vance poaching a mountain lion up near a set of caves there. Just west of that is where Jack Kincaid pulled a bloody snowball out of his pocket. Around the corner, at the head of Escarpment Creek, is where one of John Billing's guides got nabbed shooting elk in the park." On it goes, the landscape of southeast Yellowstone a kind of personal road map to a quarter century of skirmishes. Standing here it dawns on me that almost every outfitter along the southern border of the park, from upper Thorofare Creek all the way to Fox Park, has at one time or another had people working for them—or have themselves—been cited for some major offense, usually poaching. Bob claims that for some of the guides poaching is a kind of rite of passage, a way to become accepted into the club. I'm not so sure he isn't right.

It's late afternoon by the time we reach a set of meadows below Thorofare Plateau, led there not just by the work of grad student Dustin Walters, but by dots on a topo map drawn by a guide who works for one of the outfitters, now an informant. After going cross-country for a short distance we hit a back trail to the site, cut out clean as can be—cut not by axe or crosscut saw, mind you, which is of course the only legal way to do it in the wilderness, but rather by chain saw. Suddenly it's beginning to make sense why, whenever I run into certain guides, they're keenly interested in finding out where trail crews intend to travel in the coming week. "One guy actually brought in a generator," Bob says. "Set up two wall tents, one inside the other, then to dampen the noise more rigged a muffler system to expel the exhaust into a five-gallon bucket of water. Plugged in an electric chain saw, cut up his camp firewood in the middle of the night when no one was around."

Sure enough, ground into the east side of the first meadow is a circular salt site, maybe 30 yards wide, filled with fresh elk tracks—most of them made today, since this morning's rain. Pawed into the edges are three holes, each roughly the size of a garbage can lid, six to eight inches deep. I wet my finger and bring up a small amount of dirt to my tongue; there's a strong taste of salt, though how long ago it was put there is hard to say. (Depending on soil conditions, salt can stay in the ground for a long time, and elk will eat through a tremendous amount of dirt to get at it. Several guides told me they use granular salt at least every couple years, though whether that kind of frequency is actually necessary neither they nor anyone else seems to know.) From here we work our way east into a much larger meadow, where we find the granddaddy of them all—a pair of heavily trampled circles that together are roughly 50 yards long and 20 yards wide, in the middle of a meadow surrounded by burned timber. This site, too, is filled with elk tracks, mostly cows and calves—again, made earlier in the day. Bob is electrified, loving it. With the toe of his boot he etches S A L T ! into the dirt in letters two feet high. He says we should try to piece together where the shooting sites might be, so we spend a good hour circling the meadow looking for natural blinds, spent cartridges, initials carved in trees by bored hunters.

On the way back we find another trail cut out by chain saw, this one leading up to the Thorofare Plateau, where there are supposedly other sites. But evening is on us now, and given the bear factor this is no place to get caught out after dark. Making a steep fall off the ridge behind Hawks Rest we aim for a meadow close to Thorofare Creek, where from our elevated position we can see the telltale circle of yet another salt site. "This must be the one some private hunters told me about," Bob says, peering with his binoculars into a cone-shaped hole nearly 4 feet deep and 15 feet around. "You can tell they used block salt on this one, instead of the granular kind. The total area's smaller, but it's dug out deep where the block used to sit."

Only when daylight has leaked away does our conversation finally shift away from salting. Bob slides into the one other great passion of his life, which is raising buffalo in Iowa. He tells me he has the only bison ranch in the country that focuses on preserving the family herd structures that occur naturally in the wild. It's knowledge gained from observations made across more than a quarter century in Yellowstone, watching how the animals interact, thinking about the function of various behavioral traits. By keeping those family structures intact, he explains, he's been able to eliminate the need for weaning, for separating calves from cows, for creep feeding—in short, for the lion's share of what's most labor intensive about ranching. Hearing about all this leaves me less worried about the guy, knowing he'll leave Yellowstone in the fall and have this other world to put his energies to. But then I should've guessed as much.

🌿

GIVEN THE ONGOING PARADE OF VISITORS, to have even a ghost of a chance to get any writing done I'm spending much of my day hiding out in the tent—Hawks Rest West. Forty yards away, LaVoy is kind enough to play docent at the cabin, giving tours and pouring Gatorade and hot chocolate, setting out bowls of nuts and gorp. Of course, it doesn't take too many days sitting in a five-by-seven-foot backpacking tent for me to get a bad

case of cabin fever. When at last it has me by the throat I decide
to make a quick overnight to Two Ocean Pass, where I hope to
visit with some of the boys at John Winter's camp. Besides,
friends from Red Lodge are heading in this evening by horseback to Madsen's camp, located two miles up the Yellowstone,
and tomorrow they'll hike over to Hawks Rest for a visit. If
I'm going to get into the field any time soon, this 11-mile hike
is pretty much it.

Three miles from the cabin I run across one of Madsen's
guides, Jason, off his horse with packs scattered all over the place.
A hell of a wreck, he tells me, brought on when the trailing horse
in his pack string—not the sharpest tool in the shed—wrapped himself around a tree. I offer to lend a hand but he says he's got it
covered, explains that a couple of the horses are still pretty skittish, that they'd probably calm down faster with fewer people
around. Jason's a good hand, and I know of at least one Forest
Service ranger who's trying to get him to chuck the outfitting
world and become a ranger. But guides are loyal, if not always
to a single outfitter than at least to the profession. Ditching to
the other side would be like a Red Sox fan taking up with the
Yankees. Up the path a ways I find a package wrapped in a
garbage bag, determine it to be a couple of thick steaks that got
dumped in the accident. After a quick fantasy where I stuff
them into the top of my pack and eat like a king tonight, I
decide to be a good boy, carry them back down the trail and hand
them over.

"Got a couple of friends of yours coming in," Jason says,
pushing his cowboy hat up the slope of his forehead. "Should
be close behind." Sure enough, two miles farther up the trail is
the horse group with my friends Sue and Dave, both looking

remarkably fresh for having 20 miles of riding under them. Another guest of about 50 is along, too, as well as another man of roughly the same age on foot, quietly walking his pinto up the trail. There's but one company man about, a young wrangler named Matt—19 or 20 years old tops—wearing a cowboy hat and a .44 on his hip, leading two saddled horses with nobody on them. He tells me he's had an accident nine miles back; a horse reared up and fell on one of his guests, rolling over the guy's leg. He was stunned and dizzy, Matt explains, but still conscious— even tried walking for a mile or so before finally collapsing in pain. Incredibly, Matt's chosen to leave the guy sitting on the trail with his wife, fortified by nothing more than a fleece jacket and a water bottle. No one has a radio, nor is there one at Madsen's camp. Sue and Dave happened to mention that LaVoy and I had a satellite phone at Hawks Rest and so Matt has hatched a plan to make for our cabin and use that, break in if necessary. Fortunately I've got my Forest Service radio with me, and begin immediately coordinating a rescue with Teton Interagency Dispatch in Jackson—relaying information about the injured man's condition, legal descriptions of the location (Matt isn't quite sure how to figure them out from the map), whether there are any suitable landing sites for a helicopter.

My biggest immediate problem is that Forest Service radios devour batteries like grizzlies eat grubs, and halfway through the effort mine go dead. Dumb luck is on my side. Since I planned on interviewing some of John Winter's guides I've got my tape recorder along; I pluck those batteries out and thereby replace two of the nine required by the radio, and it's just enough. After hanging out for about an hour, Matt decides he needs to get his guests to camp, leaves me behind to tie up the rescue. Not until evening is well on do I finally hear from dispatch that a helicopter has touched down and whisked the injured man and his wife off to the hospital in Idaho Falls. Good news for him. Good news for me, too, since now I won't have to hike nine miles to the injured party and start a fire, wrap them in a sleeping bag to get them through the night.

As all this is going on, the guest who was leading his pinto up the trail shows up alone at Hawks Rest, still on foot, boots caked with mud from having walked through a terrible beaver bog on Atlantic Creek. He confesses to LaVoy that he's too freaked out by the accident he witnessed to get back in the saddle and ride. LaVoy tries to reassure him, tells him he's got a pretty good horse there, that he shouldn't have any problems—all to no avail. In the end all LaVoy can do is tie the reins back together (at one point the horse was standing on them and the guy solved the problem with his pocketknife), pat the man on the shoulder, and point him toward Madsen's camp. It's hard to imagine an outfit having a serious wreck with a client and then leaving him beside the trail without sleeping bag or matches or even a can of pepper spray, only to three hours later lose another guest simply by having him walk off without anyone noticing. And yet such sins are often covered by no more excuse than the attitude that life's rough in the Rockies. One operator near Open Creek actually had a habit of turning his hunting clients loose to make their own way back to the trailhead, a trip of some 40 miles, simply because he didn't want to spare either the help or the horses to send someone with them. So frequent were the complaints that the state uncharacteristically tried to revoke his permit, without success.

Having arrived at Madsen's camp somewhat late, my friend Sue oversleeps a bit the next morning. She strolls over to the cook tent at 8:30 and jokes with Nancy the cook, saying she hopes she hasn't missed breakfast. "Yep," Nancy scowls. "You sure have." Refuses to feed her, even though food is still in the serving bowls. Now I'll be the first to admit that some people are guests from hell, whining and grousing about this and that, generally making life miserable for everyone. Outfitter Warren Fleming tells of guiding a couple some years back when they spotted a female grizzly sow in a meadow playing with her cubs—truly a once-in-a-lifetime encounter. Yet this pair of dullards found the whole thing totally boring. Fleming gave them their money back, took them out the next day. But I've known Sue and Dave for years. They could be poster children for geniality—eager to learn and be a part of the group, almost obsessive about trying to follow instructions, do things right.

On returning home Sue writes a letter to Madsen, complaining about the lack of service. Madsen replies not only by calling her a liar—"I know you were told that breakfast was at 8:00 a.m."—but goes on to say that her $250 a day "did not include breakfast in bed or a butler to pick up after you." He says he spoke to his guides about the trip and they said Sue was snooty and wouldn't have anything to do with them. Which seems a bit disingenuous given that on the last morning the guides pulled their chairs under a tarp so they could eat out of a light rain, leaving their clients sitting on stumps out in the weather. "I would suggest that in the future," Madsen concludes, "you would be happiest not going on a trip of this nature. It appears that it is a little too rough for you."

When I came to Hawks Rest, it was with the naive notion that outfitters were awarded permits to make money on public lands in exchange for providing service to the public. Yet for some there's simply no circumstance under which their favorite fantasy—the one about being a rough, tough cowboy living in the wilds with scary bears—is more threatened than when dealing with summer dudes. The nonhunting summer guest is typically well heeled, well educated, and eager to know anything and everything about the land. Some might love to fish, but they also tend to be interested in history, in grizzlies, moose, and wolves. What they often get from guides are stories of danger and daring wrapped in long diatribes about how evil wolves are, how grizzlies are overrunning the wilderness. It's a telling scene when one of Madsen's wranglers, listening to a guest tell of a mountain climber making a difficult ascent at 25,000 feet, shakes his head in genuine confusion. "I don't get it," he says. "Why would you go to a place like that? No fishing to be had, nothing to hunt."

There are splendid exceptions, of course. Like longtime outfitter Press Stephens, past president of the Wyoming Outfitters and Guides Association. Having for years worked as a hunting guide, Stephens has left that behind to focus instead on people seeking other kinds of wilderness experiences. His educational and wildlife-watching treks are incredibly popular, and this year his Yellowstone trips are booked all the way through the third week in October. "The clients may have more trouble getting in here than they did 20 years ago," says Stephens. "They're using muscles that in this day and age don't get used as much. The upside, though, is that they care more about the resource." Stephens is one of less than a handful of outfitters who eagerly practices no-trace horse packing—a movement he says exists in large part thanks to the Park Service. "We all got together and started trying to figure out new ways of doing things. Today I can have 20 horses in this camp, and after we leave you'd never know we were here." He says clients today understand and appreciate those efforts, whereas 20 years ago "they would've thought I was goofy, absolutely insane. Back then the thinking was that God put trees here to tie horses to."

Not everyone is impressed. "He's just not one of us anymore," complains guide Blaine Gilliand. "He wears a baseball hat. He went from being critical of the wolf reintroduction before it happened to being mildly okay with it." Which to Gilliand is proof that Stephens is "wishy-washy." (Needless to say, had Press gone the other way, from being okay with wolves to now being against them, he'd at last be sitting squarely on the pillars of wisdom.) "It's not that he's against hunting, or anything like that," Blaine concludes. "It's that he turned his back on the cowboy way."

There are few jobs more demanding than that of an outfitter. Look at the fingers of most men in this profession and you'll find painful-looking cracks from blood and water freezing in them during the frigid days of autumn. Per capita there must be more frostbitten toes and noses, more bruises and broken bones than in almost any other profession short of stuntman and linebacker. It requires tremendous skill and stamina to maneuver a string of horses or mules month after month through the backcountry, staying upright through lousy weather and skittish animals and ornery bears. A great many are aware on some level of being surrounded by astonishing beauty, even if they don't realize it's probably the beauty that takes the edge off whatever foolishness may rise in the face of too much whiskey, too many grizzlies, too many guns. In all it's a rich and proud tradition, a major thread in the history of the American West. What's more, most clients never hear the part about the lousy pay guides receive, about the outfitter being in debt up to his ears, the fact that liability insurance is way up and the vet bills are sky-high and his kid needs braces and the whole damned summer trade just might sink if fishing doesn't get better in the upper Yellowstone.

As many claim, this may well be a passing way of life. But only in its current form. There will always be people entranced by wilderness, wanting and needing to go there whether or not their particular hungers happen to match those of the cowboy way. Compared to the brutal finality with which the native way of life was extinguished 150 years ago, the transformation we're talking about is a visit to the candy store. And yet I'm constantly amazed at the degree to which outfitters are wrapped in a victim mentality. Emerging from this profession, at least in the Thorofare, is a mean-spirited paranoia, a constant griping about wolves and city people and antihunting groups destroying a way of life; in short, it's become one of the most self-indulgent whinefests ever to unfurl in the land of the Great Divide. Of course there's nothing inherently wrong with choosing to go down in flames instead of adapting to new conditions, electing to hold fast to the fantasy of dime-store novels instead of planting some scrap of those dreams in the real world. That sort of choice has been made many times throughout history. But how much more dignity there would be—and who knows, perhaps even a small victory now and then—if the struggles were fueled by those things that make the life of an outfitter truly inspiring, rather than by that which makes him most uncertain and afraid.

ALREADY WE'RE HALFWAY THROUGH the second week of August.
With the mosquitoes finally gone and the weather fine, as of late
I've taken to writing outside again—the Crazy Creek chair laid
out west of the hitching posts, my legs outstretched on either side
of that big stump. A loose cluster of mature lodgepole pine sur-
rounds the site, and through the trees directly in front of me is
an incredible view of the rim of Two Ocean Plateau and the
Falcon Creek drainage. Slightly to my left, meanwhile, I can look
beyond two large, seven-foot-high boulders sitting in the pasture,
over long tongues of willow toward Atlantic Creek. A recent cold
front brought blustery winds and nighttime temperatures in the
20s, washing the air clean of smoke and haze; morning skies are
clear and bright, though already they're showing the darker,
richer hues of autumn.

Only last week the plants of the tundra were still rushing
to bloom, playing catch-up to the low country, as they've been
doing since spring first broke along the Yellowstone in early June.
No more. The bloom that spilled across the high ridges and
plateaus has come to an end, ground to a halt by frost, turning
the leaves of cushion plants to rust and orange and red. From
now on it's the highlands that will lead the season, rushing
headlong toward autumn, with the lower forests and the meadows along the Yellowstone falling a day, two days, a week behind.
Gone is the illusion that summer has somehow broken free, that
it's no longer tethered to the same rhythms that bind winter and
fall and spring.

There are different smells now—dust instead of dampness,
a thin sweetness from curing grass instead of the perfume of
lupine and rose. But for the persistent bog created by beavers
working the lower sections of Atlantic Creek, the trails are dry,

free of the sucking mud that once grabbed at horse's hooves and hiker's boots. The meadows are all cinnamon and butternut, only the willow holding onto shades of green. Asters, harebells, and gentians are still in bloom, and in shaded, wet places sticky geraniums; the fireweed is holding up well but looking ragged, the heads of the stalks missing more and more petals with every passing day. In the lowlands, strawberries and whortleberries are heavy with fruit, swelled by a season of decent rains, soon to be vacuumed away by black bears and grizzlies—a juicy, sugar-rich appetizer that marks the front end of a hyperactive feeding phase that will run all the way through fall.

The fishermen have mostly left, bound again for Turpin Meadow, their panniers full of tents and camp chairs and empty bottles of Jose Cuervo and George Dickel, the horses and mules moving at a faster clip now, knowing full well that this is the direction that leads toward home. As people leave the wildlife returns. Bridger Lake is nearly silent, and with every dawn comes the chance for us to walk the shoreline and spot a remarkably array of creatures, from otters to kingfishers to moose, as well as the whole bald eagle family, their two kids finally on the wing, scouring the waters for the flash of cutthroat. There are cinnamon teals and muskrat and Canada geese on the water; on most mornings, sitting above it all in the most noble of poses, a great blue heron perches high on the branch of a burned tree.

The kids of the Wyoming Wilderness Academy are readying to leave too, stopping by the cabin one more time to fill their cowboy hats with handfuls of candy. With them always these days is Joseph, a grinning, slightly overweight Hispanic kid of 16 from downtown Los Angeles. His dad is fresh out of prison, Dann Harvey tells me, drifting, while mom has only limited visitation because she's still hooked on drugs. Which leaves Joseph living in a group home. This trip to the Teton Wilderness is the first time he's ever been out of L.A.–first time out of range of drive-bys and drugs, of the expensive metal detectors he says sit just inside the doors of the high school. When Joseph first arrived at Hawks Rest, I remember him being like many kids half afraid of the place, nervous, stiff in the saddle. Now he's utterly alive. Most afternoons he spends hours playing with the younger kids, launching rounds of hide-and-seek, singing songs with them. "I really wanna come back here next year," he tells me, sitting tall in the saddle outside the tack room. "Get back here with these horses."

From what we can figure the Delta wolf pack is 16 animals, though less than a handful ever come south out of the park to cruise the riverbanks in front of the cabin. The other adults hunt either to the west on Two Ocean Plateau or move eastward up Mountain, Howell, Escarpment, Cliff, and Beaver Creeks. While some adults make their hunting forays, others still care for pups at the rendezvous site, well north of the den and wrapped in thick walls of willow. A safe and quiet location. Quiet, that is, until grizzlies come around.

With the exception of Mollie's pack, located in the bear-rich meadows of Pelican Valley, no other group is having more interactions with grizzlies than this one. During a tracking flight this week, head wolf biologist Doug Smith watches as a grizzly stumbles into the rendezvous site—attracted, perhaps, by the scent of elk carcasses lying about from previous kills. As the bear moves through the willows, the adults take up what has by now become somewhat of a routine. Several wolves come in close to the bruin, at times a mere eight or ten feet away, circling and yapping, never for a minute leaving it alone. For his part the bear doesn't even bother to swat at them, having no doubt learned that while he may be far stronger, he's no match for their quickness. Slapping and lunging is simply a waste of energy. The scene turns frenzied, Smith tells us, when a pup blunders to within six feet of the bear, leaving some of the adults trying to marshal him and his siblings to safety while the rest of the pack continues to swirl. "They can't force a bear out," he explains, "but they can definitely harass it. And they'll keep that up as long as the grizzly remains anywhere within a hundred yards of the site." Every time the outcome is the same. The bear decides it's too much trouble to stay around, and when he turns to leave the wolves are always right behind, ushering him out. On another day this summer, in an even more remarkable scene, when Mr. Bear finally tired of being harassed and turned to leave, Smith watched a Delta wolf run after him and bite him on the butt.

While on most days elk from the area are high up on Two Ocean Plateau, on occasion they drift back down to hang in the valley, often near Falcon Creek in an area burned just last year. Thanks to that fire, not only is the place flush with plants, but the nutrient level in their leaves is considerably higher than in vegetation in places that never saw flame. On several occasions horsemen have spooked the elk and sent well over a hundred animals pounding up the mountain. In all it's a circumstance that proves a boon for the Delta pack, allowing easy hunting from both the den as well as the rendezvous site.

On August 10 we look north from Hawks Rest into Yellowstone to see a large plume of smoke burning on a side hill near Phlox Creek; we get on the radio quick and make a report to Teton Interagency Dispatch. It's one of more than 30 lightning-caused fires that will burn in the park this summer, and in another week winds from the east will begin churning hard, eventually pushing the fire from 78 acres to just over 3,600. By August 16 the smoke will be so bad that Bob Jackson won't be able to get into the Thorofare cabin from the Ninemile Trailhead; meanwhile, an outfitter, his guests, and several private parties in the southern reaches of Yellowstone Park join forces and ride hard to the north, choking on smoke. Shortly after their retreat flames cross the meadows and jump the river to the east side of the valley, shutting down a large section of the Thorofare Trail along with 15 backcountry campsites.

That night we stand in front of the cabin and watch dozens of spot fires burning in the foothills around Phlox Creek, great pulses of orange light bouncing off the bottoms of the clouds near Two Ocean Plateau. Given how quickly the blaze is advancing, I can't help but wonder what the place must have looked like back in 1988, with fuel moisture barely a third of what it is today, and winds far stronger still. Day and night across the valley come loud cracking noises as trees burned 14 years ago fall before the winds. Not once in the next two weeks will I leave the cabin without taking note of the breeze on my face, knowing full well that a shift to the north could leave us making a hasty retreat to escape the flames.

In the midst of all this, a few backpacking parties are finally strolling through, one diverted some 30 miles off its intended route by the fires. A surprising number complain about being scowled at by guides on horseback, find little comfort when I tell them such greetings are fairly common. It isn't just clubbiness or territorialism that rankles the boys when they spot foot travelers coming up the trail. As a group backpackers have for some become symbols of the enemy—liberal tree-huggers who'd like nothing better than to kick ranchers and outfitters off the land and fill the countryside with wolves. Meanwhile, some backpackers are fairly good at scowling themselves, seeing horses as terrible beasts who do little but graze the hell out of the meadows and turn trails into mudholes.

While the debate about the pros and cons of pack stock isn't always rancorous, it extends on occasion even to rangers and trail workers. Most wouldn't trade a good mule for a million bucks, while others seem less convinced. "For me stock makes it seem less like a wilderness experience," explains Kate, a trail crew worker who's been living and working with horses and mules all summer long. "They're your eyes and ears. They allow you to relax more, and that's not necessarily a good thing." She's also not fond of bells going off all night, says that with stock in camp most other wildlife won't come anywhere near.

But Kate's in the minority. Her work partner, Darren, feels exactly the opposite, loving not just the craft of horsemanship, but that so many things can go wrong. "With horses trouble can come on fast," he explains. "That leaves me feeling like I'm living on the edge." Frank Deluka of Yellowstone, meanwhile, has a somewhat middle-of-the-road perspective, saying how he really appreciates what horses can do for him, but that he grew up backpacking, and pack animals have moved him out of a mentality based on economy and self-sufficiency. "I've gotten to the place where I throw all kinds of stuff on the packhorse. I've got a Walkman at the cabin now and food for 15 days, even though I only need enough for five. I'm not convinced that's good for me."

In truth, there are few forests in the nation that use pack strings as extensively as the Shoshone and Bridger-Teton, and much of the work that gets done here simply wouldn't happen without them. Pack animals haul an incredible variety of supplies, from the kitchen cabinets at Hawks Rest cabin to bridge timbers and posts, gravel and concrete, food and feed, and axes and cross-cut saws—some of it in panniers, the rest secured in tarps and atop saddles using a complex set of rope hitches. The six-mule strings commonly used here can carry roughly 1,500 pounds, much more over short distances. (Unlike horses, which carry roughly 65 percent of their weight on their front legs, a mule's body weight is more evenly distributed, which tends to make them more sure-footed.)

As I've already suggested, not having my own pack stock makes me highly suspect among my neighbors, sort of like a guy living in Detroit and driving a Volvo. Yet all through August the pilgrimages to our cabin by horsemen continue—in large part because word is out that I'm writing a book; there are plenty of people eager to hand me the real skinny about how things work in this wilderness. With the bourbon or the coffee comes big help-ings of coaxing and arm-twisting about everything from salting to wolves, pontifications that would do any Jehovah Witness proud. Bob Jackson's a regular, as are several guides from sur-rounding camps. One afternoon outfitter BJ Hill stops in with hunting guide Blaine Gilliand. BJ wastes no time pulling out a bottle of peach brandy, settling himself into the old director's chair to spin me a few lessons.

A lot of what's going on with regard to wilderness these days is clearly driving BJ nuts. He's fearful of nature lovers who want to stop all sport hunting, says they don't realize that given the limits of winter range such a move would cause regular mass starvations. He's concerned that seven years ago wolf supporters agreed that once recovered the population would need to be controlled at the edges of the ecosystem, and now he sees them backpedaling. BJ's trying hard to be on his best behavior, treating me, I suspect, a little like he says you have to treat the environmentalists who show up in Jackson wanting to shut down the elk refuge. "No matter what the truth is," he explains, "you always want to read a little bit of liberalism into it, just to keep 'em calmed down." He mentions Harold Turner of the Triangle X as being one of the great negotiators—never making himself look bad and never ever giving the environmentalists the full scheme of things. "Plain and simple," BJ says, passing me the bottle of brandy, "if you sit down and tell the facts directly, how it really is, then you throw the rest of America clear off." Outfitters need to get on the page, he adds—stop doing things like salting or leaving unsightly carcass piles that could bring negative attention to the industry. Throughout the conversation I get the sense such assertions aren't being offered so much in the spirit of there being anything wrong with those old ways, so much as from a reluctant acceptance that it's the outsiders who are spinning the world. "The Merideth Taylors [of the Wyoming Outdoor Council] and the Bob Jacksons won't allow things to continue," he explains. "These outfitters have to tow the line or somebody's gonna take them down. It's not 1970 or 1980 anymore."

If environmentalists are good at spin, BJ himself is no slacker. Turning to the controversy about shutting down artificial feeding in the National Elk Refuge, he presents it not from the perspective of what it could do to outfitters, but to the grizzlies. "Once they take away the feeding on the refuge, the other 22 state feed grounds around Jackson will be vulnerable to the same problem. Pretty soon you drop from, say, 40,000 head of elk to a natural winter range that can hold 15,000. Lose those elk and the grizzlies in this ecosystem won't survive." You just can't remove from the food chain that many elk calves, he says—and in the fall, gut piles—and expect the bears to make it. Though most environmentalists aren't really talking about closing the refuge, but rather reducing the 2,500 tons of alfalfa put out as feed in a given year—which would indeed mean fewer elk—BJ's right about the importance of elk to bears. Especially in greater Yellowstone, where nearly 80 percent of the diet of adult males and almost half that of female grizzlies is meat. (Compare this to Glacier National Park, where fully 95 percent of the diet of both sexes is plant matter.) Around these parts, there's no getting around the fact that elk provide one of the highest sources of digestible energy available.

At the mere mention of bears, Blaine breaks from a separate conversation with LaVoy. "Here's the problem with this whole grizzly thing," he says. "There isn't enough habitat to support what we've got. When October comes these big, hungry, oversize bruins really suffer, especially in a bad year when the whitebark pine nuts aren't there. It's almost sad to watch the things come into your camp every day and just stand around, trying to figure any way just to get something to eat. They're eating the horse shit on our trails. The poor bastards are hungry. Without the gut piles hunters leave in the fall, they'd be in real trouble." While on the surface such comments can seem generous—and over the course of the summer I've heard them countless times—in general, concern for bears among hunters seems a mile wide and an inch deep. At one point—maybe it's the brandy talking—I joke to Blaine and BJ that with carcasses and gut piles being so important to grizzlies we should take our hats off to the wolves, since their kills are leaving thousands of pounds of meat across the ecosystem—carcasses available not just during hunting season, but throughout the year.

It takes a while for the cursing to stop. Once again the mere mention of wolves has had a stirring effect on our guests, making even BJ Hill give up the spin campaign. He takes another swig of brandy, looks around the room like he barely knows where to start. First of all, he offers, we're dealing with a Canadian wolf. "When I sit at Mammoth and look at that stuffed American wolf they've got up there, versus what's been introduced, I say somethin' ain't right here. Do we really know how ungulates in the lower 48 are going to react—how they'll handle a species that wasn't here in the first place so to speak?" He goes on to explain that the wolves we ended up getting are sport killers, and that this has been amply proven over the last two years in the Gros Ventre Range, where he says wolves have been wounding elk for fun and tearing their lips off. The whole damn thing, he assures me, is unfolding exactly as the older outfitters predicted it would. As for why the hunting has remained so good in the Thorofare, that's all bound to change.

Wolf conversations lead almost without exception to comments about the damn out-of-staters—in particular the horrible Easterners, which always strikes me as a little odd given that most hunting clients are from there. They're downtown New Yorkers, says BJ about the people behind the push for wolves. "Stuck in traffic every day. They like the idea of a kind of American Serengeti out here, but we just can't live that way." At which point Blaine caps the brandy, sticks it in his pocket, and stands to leave. "They think we're going to go away," he says. "But all they're really going to do is make outlaws out of us. They think we're going to change–that we're gonna quit hunting, that we're gonna quit guiding to preserve what they think needs to be preserved. But they're wrong."

BJ nods his approval. "In Wyoming there's 550,000 independent people and every one of them has their own niche in this state. Right or wrong, we'll be a long time changing."

It might seem odd that a discussion of wolves would end in a spirited defense of the homeland. The important thing to understand is that the truly fierce reactions have less to do with wolves per se than with the government that reintroduced them. Again, ranchers and many other rural people throughout the intermountain West have felt for a long time as if the world is turning against them. Meatpacking monopolies have kept beef prices in the toilet for years. Subdivisions are spreading faster than knapweed, bringing higher taxes, not to mention newcomers who sometimes can't abide much at all about rural life, from the sound of tractors at six in the morning, to cattle snacking on public lands. Just as bad for outfitters is the fact that their hunting clients are aging, the younger generation showing little interest in the sport. "A family pulls into my base camp down there to ride horses," says BJ. "The parents wanna ride and the kids wanna sit in the goddamn car. Some overweight kid, sitting there in tennis shoes and an earring in his ear. That kid's gonna be running this country in 20 years, and he's gonna be antihunting to the max."

"Either that," Blaine adds, "or else the guy's married to an antihunter-type little gal who thinks it's not cool to kill Bambi. The average age of our hunters is about 54–we're not getting new ones. Maybe a client will bring his kid along one time, but that's it."

In short, the wolf is larger than life in Wyoming because it's the symbol of all that's gone wrong with the world. Like any recipe heavy with loathing and disgust, this is a dish in great need of powerful symbols—stirring, incendiary images that can upset and arouse. And throughout history no token has been relied on more often to define a wide range of disparate evils than the wolf. The Catholics figured that out about 800 years ago, when, eager to find a kind of spiritual cattle prod to scare the faithful into obedience, they chose the wolf, declaring it to be literally the devil's dog, proof of Satan walking the Earth.

It worked then for many of the same reasons it works today. At the time forests throughout much of northern Europe were being cut over to make way for agriculture. Deer and other ungulate populations were faltering, which in turn sent all kinds of predators into the countryside to make their living on livestock. Highly skilled in theatrics, the church not only singled out the wolf as the critter everyone would love to hate, but also began burning them at the stake; that, or cutting off their snouts while the animals were still alive and placing wigs on their heads—an act meant to make them more closely resemble some evil person who lived in earlier times, said to have returned to Earth from the depths of hell in a wolf suit—finally hanging them in the village square. Forget tales of Romulus and Remus, whose little butts were saved by wolves. And never mind that many Native American cultures say they actually patterned their society after wolves—in part due to the loose style of governance used by the alpha male and female, as well as for the staunch loyalty among pack members, especially their devotion to the young.

Rural people today need devils no less than the next guy. (Actually, it's a bit unfair to assign such perspective only to those living in the sticks. Following the rape of a jogger in Central Park in the spring of 1989, regional and national tabloids employed animal images a whopping 185 times, making frequent comparisons between the rapists and a pack of wolves.) Three hundred years after storytellers changed the wolf in Little Red Riding Hood from a creature who actually slept with Little Red to a bloodthirsty killer, we continued to spend millions of dollars each year to keep the things from ending life as we know it. Long after biologists realized the value of predators in a healthy ecosystem, men fresh back from the Second World War were gunning down wolves in Minnesota and northern Michigan—"hunting Nazis," as the practice was affectionately known.

"Maybe we need predators and tyrants nibbling around the flanks of our flocks and families, to challenge us to rebuild the fortifications and sharpen our marksmanship." So thinks Gary Marbut of the Montana Shooting Sports Association. "But the predators against whom we must fortify are those among our own kind who are comfortable seeing us as prey, those who would threaten the survival of our freedoms for their own whims, the would-be tyrants who would prey upon our liberties to serve their own agendas. Would these same supporters send their children to play in the forests and hills where real, live, hungry, flesh-eating wolves actually roam? Only if they are so genetically removed from man's heritage that they have lost all personal survival instinct." More proof still that no people are more addicted to the apocryphal than we of the golden West.

CHAPTER NINE

*S*AL, THE CABIN TENDER AT FOX PARK, HAS hiked the 12 miles from his abode on the upper Snake River to hang out with us for a couple of days here at Hawks Rest. Two hours after his arrival comes seasonal Cynthia Wolf, riding up with a full complement of horses and mules and an Australian shepherd named Lash Larue. Sal is 39 and six years ago he gave up a good paying job as an environmental engineer to work odd jobs and roam the world. So far he's done a pretty good job of it, having landed stints doing everything from washing dishes in Antarctica to serving as a deckhand on a 50-foot sloop in the Caribbean. He's written one novel, has two more in the works, and cooks like Wolfgang Puck. Cynthia, meanwhile, has been coming to the Thorofare country for more than a decade, usually preferring to work alone as an independent contractor. She describes herself as homeless, currently in possession of five horses and mules, two dogs, a truck, and a horse trailer. They sit around the table over plates of spaghetti and talk of being the black sheep and misfits of their families, celebrating that distinction with no less pleasure than the handful of cowboys across the meadow squeeze from slamming back bourbon and relishing the feel of their guns.

Like Lone Eagle Woman, like the fine old hippie writer and ranger Mike Wolcott down in Nowlin Meadow—who says he wants to author a book called "If a Vagrant Rants in the Woods, Does Anyone Hear?"—these are the other people who spend extended amounts of time in this, the most remote place in the United States. There are far fewer of them, and finding each other can be like stumbling across a fellow castaway at the far end of the island. For the most part they were born and bred in mainstream America, but by either blessing or curse found no lasting reward there. They're remarkably bright, though by their own admission are slow learners—stumbling often, needing both space and time to figure things out, wandering always, but rarely lost. Some writers have been critical of such types, pointing out what at first glance seems hypocritical. On one hand, say the pundits, such backcountry bohemians despise Americans' obsession with independence and self-centeredness, all the while indulging their own need to be alone in the wilds. But there's a difference between the kind of individualism used to climb the ladder of success and win nifty prizes and the kind applied in the boondocks, which at least on good days can serve as a path to both self-knowledge and self-reliance. This is not *Survivor*. While society may reward the narcissist, the wilderness—the real one, that is—will kill him.

I recall similar talk in our first days at Hawks Rest, in that time spent with those kind, unfortunate friends who ended up neck-deep in the Zen task of helping us reclaim the cabin from the grease and the rodents. The poet and professor of the pair, Jim Peterson, now in his early 50s and a relative newcomer to the wild, told us on that first night he'd come on this trek from his home in Virginia in part to see if it was possible to unleash some deeper sense of self-reliance. Not that he's planning to move to the outback. Rather, that in the outback were found the metaphors he needed for a more authentic way of living. "Everybody in our culture is worried about dying in the poorhouse, losing it all, as if those things were really doing anything for them. That's a massive illusion. To have an understanding that even if we lost everything we had there'd still be a way to function, to live—that's a lesson nature can teach." Like a lot of bright academics, Jim admits his tendency to intellectualize everything. "It's easy to have things all nice and neat in your head, read your Buddhism and Hinduism and Christianity texts, sit back in the safety of your home and think you're living those ideas. But getting it in your head is only the beginning. Wilderness forces you to start living your philosophy. It comes out in the way you treat the land, treat the people you're with. How you handle the stress of everything from mosquitoes to grizzly bears. How you treat yourself."

Near dark come still more visitors, as another trail crew sidles up to the hitching posts. In the lead is Darren, back from several months spent in Baltimore, where he tried on the big city life for a while, found it didn't fit. And Kate, her long, blond hair hanging in pigtails around her smudged face, here in the wilderness as part of an internship for Oregon State University. And finally Justin—a strapping man from Riverton, Wyoming, who started cowboying when he was 13, breaking horses, and has been doing so ever since. For a time he was ranch foreman on the giant IX Ranch in the Bear Paw Mountains of northern Montana; he's pushed cows all over Wyoming, even eastern Washington. Remarkably he's never broken a bone, though at 31 he already has severe tendonitis from a feast of wrecks, the latest being three days ago when a big mare rolled over him. He's an artist, too, a sculptor, and in the winter months works at a foundry in Lander. Justin wants one day to move into art full time, but the horses and the cattle just won't leave him alone. "I'll get into the art as soon as I get this cowboying thing out of my system," he says over a plate heaped high with spaghetti.

"Like you're going to get that out of your system," Kate says.

It's hard to find a job cowboying anymore, Justin tells us. For one thing, in a lot of places four-wheelers have taken over for the horse. Besides, there's not much money in ranching, and kids 18 or 19 don't necessarily want to follow in their family's footsteps, figuring they can make a lot better wages somewhere else. Justin says even when he does land a good ranch job, it's tough to find a place where he can take his girls, ages 10 and 12, since more and more insurance companies are refusing to allow family members to be around company livestock. "They don't even like a cowboy to have his own horse anymore," he explains sadly. "They don't want to be responsible for injuries the horse might get from the stock. If I could do my art, cowboy, and be with my girls, that would be a great life." Noticeably absent from his wish list is his wife of 12 years, a policewoman in a small town in Wyoming. The two are in the middle of a trial separation. "One of the reasons I took this job was to get some distance, get on a horse, and be in a place where I could think things out."

If things don't work out, I think to myself, maybe Justin could track down Allison Fay Smith of California, who 30 years ago sent the following letter to the supervisor of the Teton National Forest:

> Gentlemen:
>
> To explain the situation briefly: I am employed as a secretary but would prefer working outdoors in the clean fresh air far away from the smog and confusion of suburban life.
>
> Have you any (decent) rangers who are looking for a wife? I am a staunch Catholic, never married before, 25 years old. My friends consider me fairly attractive.
>
> Having managed a house for my family of nine for several years, I am capable of cooking, sewing, and doing the necessary domestic chores. My hobbies include hiking, camping, horseback riding, swimming, and reading.
>
> If you have anyone interested in further correspondence, please write to ...

To which the supervisor replied:

> Dear Miss Smith:
>
> Thank you for your recent letter inquiring as to whether we employ any Rangers that are looking for a wife. Unfortunately, at the present time we have no single Rangers, decent or otherwise.
>
> We are forwarding your letter to Grand Teton

National Park for reply as you have also addressed
it to Jenny Lake Ranger Station.

Thank you for your interest in the Teton
National Forest.

The evening winds down with this crew, like so many
others, lamenting the fact that they have no real authority in this
wilderness. In truth their situation is exactly how Frank Deluka
describes working for the Forest Service south of here, in the
Wind River Range. "We had one law enforcement guy in
the whole region," Frank recalls, "and everybody knew it. If I
wrote a ticket to somebody they could tear it up in my face and
the only thing I could do was to call in our one law enforcement
officer, who might have to travel some 30 miles by horse to get
here. Of course that never happened." Frank says the problem
was especially bad for foot rangers, who routinely had outfitters ignore them, refuse even to speak to them let alone stop and
show their permits. "That, or else they'd see you coming at the
far end of a meadow and simply head another way, knowing full
well you couldn't catch up to them on foot." As for approaching
hunting camps to do compliance checks, "with 15 half-drunk
guys with guns, well, the consensus was that none of us should
be doing that."

Such conditions are part and parcel of a larger issue among
some seasonals of simply not feeling supported. Budget con-
straints aside, these workers are well aware that, at least from the
supervisor's office on up, life is a highly political game; if sticking to the rules makes life difficult for a powerful constituency
like the outfitters, plain and simple meaningful enforcement—
something beyond token citations—isn't going to happen. Though

it's true that tickets stacking up in their files is enough to give some outfitters pause, it's also true that for a permit to actually be pulled is almost unheard of. Against this background many Forest Service employees, including even some permanent staff, either get frustrated and give up, or more often, try to satisfy themselves with the knowledge that at least they're keeping trails in order and campsites clean, that their presence may provide some small incentive for complying with important matters like food storage. As far as the chance of the agency ever creating a situation where everyone is playing by the same rules, most seem to consider that a pipe dream. "The Forest Service tends to do the right thing," former district ranger Don Hooper told me once, "mostly when someone from the public shines a big spotlight on them."

LaVoy and I continue to spend our days dancing with various projects: replacing faucets and leaks in the plumbing system, digging out the spring box yet again, cutting fallen timber from the trails around Bridger Lake, splitting firewood for the Forest Service crews soon to arrive for fall patrol. In the last week of August there come again rumblings of hooves on the bridge in front of the cabin, as horsemen head in to set up hunting camps. Nate Vance is up Open Creek with his team of strapping mules, while Eldredge Perry is hauling loads into Blind Basin. Madsen's boys are busy cutting seven cords of wood with crosscut saws—"the worst part of the job," one wrangler tells me, looking exhausted by the mere thought of it—while the Turners are gearing up their dynasty on the other side of Two Ocean Plateau. In all there will be hundreds of hunters in these northern reaches of the wilderness, every one of them here for a shot at a large bull. Some will be blue-collar workers from Michigan and New Jersey, having saved up years for what they imagine will be the hunt of a lifetime. More common still will be doctors, attorneys, software designers, detectives, and the like. (When all hell broke loose on 9/11, the No. two man for the Secret Service was here, in a hunting camp at Two Ocean Pass.)

With hunting season approaching, the volume of wolf rhetoric gets turned up louder, though most of the comments now focus on how wolves tend to move the elk. Guides are imagining long days spent locating trophies for their clients, only to have their work go bust as an eager hunter crawls over the lip of a rise for the big shot and finds only empty meadows below. "Of course they don't like it," one avid private hunter tells me. "It means they have to actually hunt." Bow hunting guides seem even more frustrated. Their hunters, after all, depend on drawing in bulls by trading bugle calls; when wolves are around, they explain, bugling goes way down, only to pick up again once the pack finally leaves.

After more than two months and some 300 miles of walking, LaVoy and I are about to part company. He's leaving the backcountry altogether, walking south to Turpin Meadow and then driving west to Idaho, where he'll catch a float trip down the Salmon River with a group of at-risk kids. As for me, I'll be staying on at Hawks Rest for another couple of weeks, then hiking out eastward across the Absaroka divide. We've decided to make a last quick journey together, climbing out of the Yellowstone meadows to Phelps Pass, then southward across Two Ocean Plateau to the Parting of the Waters. There's been a cloud of melancholy hanging over the cabin. Several times in the past week I've noticed LaVoy sitting on his bunk staring at nothing in particular, his normally bright gaze dimmed, the corners of his mouth sagging behind nine weeks worth of beard. Friends from Red Lodge who've been visiting for the past two days decide to forgo hiking out with us and head off in the opposite direction, toward Woodard Pass.

And that's probably a good thing. There's a certain comfort in the two of us being able to walk out quietly, knowing without a word the right time to turn back for a final look at the cabin through the burned trees along Falcon Creek. When to glance at a certain cave on the sheer face of Hawks Rest, where a week ago we sat and watched a marsh hawk hunting, saw a cow moose and calf loping through the grass, their black coats shining in the sun. When to look for those young eagles of Bridger Lake, or grab a view of that flat shin of The Trident where we once sat waiting for wolves. Our summer together has been a story. And while much of that tale turned on the antics of outfitters and rangers and trail crews, underneath it always was the land itself–this fine and rambling medley of promontories and wet meadows and bends in the river.

Part way up Phelps Pass, overlooking the valley of the upper Yellowstone, I'm suddenly filled with a feeling that first showed up when I was just a kid–a sensation peculiar to summer, when I'd wake up and peer out the small window at the foot of my bed onto sunlight dripping across the yard, knowing as sure as I breathed that there was some great adventure waiting beyond that back fence. Today that same sensation is flooding back–not as a memory per se, but as if the past has found the present. As if those times as a kid were part joy in the moment

and part premonition, an awareness that one day there would
be a fine morning just like this one, in some distant place well
to the west, in a summer far away.

We'd planned to head west as far as Fox Park, stay the night
in the Forest Service patrol cabin, but the mere thought of Two
Ocean Plateau is so compelling that at the last minute we scrap
that idea and begin the final thousand-foot climb to the tundra.
The soil is parched and the grasses withered, bent and rusted by
a run of heavy frosts. There's little sign of elk and therefore little sign of wolves; tomorrow an outfitter will tell me that after
60 miles of riding, all the way to the windswept eastern boundary of the forest, as well as into the southern reaches of the park,
he saw nothing in the way of elk, as if thousands of them had
vanished from the face of the Earth. It is spectacularly lonesome.
To the west the Tetons rip into the western sky, climbing with
such ferocity that it seems the scene should be attended by
drums and shouts. And yet nothing fills our ears but the roar of
a cold, hard wind.

The next morning, after barely 30 minutes of walking and
long before we're ready, the trail begins dropping fast toward Two
Ocean Creek. Though we'd originally planned three days out,
I know now we'll have less than two, that I'll say my farewells
and head back north in midafternoon, making Hawks Rest by
early evening. Which is how it happens, stopping first to take
pictures of each other standing barefoot at the Parting of the
Waters, straddling a nearly imperceptible ridge of the Continental
Divide. One leg planted in Atlantic Creek, which from here is
more than 3,400 miles from its namesake ocean, another planted
in Pacific Creek, which is itself some 1,300 miles from the sea.
"I'll do my crying on the trail," LaVoy tells me after a big hug.

I stand there watching him walk off to the west, and not once does he look back. Keep jumping, you old mouse, I think to myself, wishing I'd thought of it in time to say it to his face.

Before heading back to Hawks Rest I stop in at John Winter's camp, visit with Blaine and Judd and some of the boys. Blaine's fresh off a three-day trip that included a spectacular horse wreck a mile or so up Bruin Creek. "I was heading down the mountain to shoot the horses," he says, thinking the animals surely crippled. "But there they were, standing at the bottom, shaking." By the time he recovered and repacked, led them out, and made it back to camp it was two o'clock in the morning. He tells me there are lots of bears running around up there, including one that long-time outfitter John Winter said was the biggest he's ever seen. I tell him this isn't great news, given that pretty soon I'll be heading home up that very drainage. "Don't be too concerned," Blaine says. "It's not the big ones you have to worry about."

Blaine's been busy hatching theories, which in truth is among the most respectable of activities for anyone who spends long periods of time in the wild. Early in the 19th century trapper James Clyman was weaving ideas about the speed of light, while his contemporary Rufus Sage busied himself comparing the Sioux language with Latin, postulating that at some point the Romans must have showed up on the plains and handed off their language to the natives. Bob Jackson has the whole group dynamics of buffalo going on in his head, while LaVoy as of late has been chewing on matters of evolution—in particular, the notion that as a species we started struggling emotionally at the point we were able to conceive a future. Blaine's inner work, meanwhile, trends a bit more toward the practical. It has to do with the idea that the tons of berries grizzlies are eating right now are important to them not so much as a food source, but as a scouring agent, a purgative, ridding the bears of intestinal bugs before the onset of the fall feeding frenzy. No biologist I've talked to has even considered such a thing. But as far as Blaine's concerned, that doesn't make it any less likely.

On leaving Winter's camp I find myself hurrying down the trail, disheartened by the fact that my own leaving is so close at hand. Late in the afternoon, some three miles out from Hawks Rest, in a quiet patch of broken forest, I hear a slight rustling off to my left. Directly beside me, not 30 yards away, is a very large chocolate-colored grizzly—head down, digging with enthusiasm around the base of a lodgepole pine, scooping mouthfuls of grubs or ants or God knows what. I couldn't have spent this much time in grizzly country without imagining such a scenario, chewing on theories about whether it would be best to shout, or just stand there and try to look big, or just turn back quietly and go the other way. My can of pepper spray comes out fast, the trigger lock knocked away. Remarkably, the bear remains oblivious. Even more astonishing is that I find myself admiring how good he looks—the fat on his body, his thick, glossy coat.

I manage to increase the space between us by moving slowly sideways up a hill covered in bunchgrass and fireweed, watching him with my pack turned slightly so that should he suddenly look up, my skinny ass will look bigger than it really is. With every step the dry vegetation gives a slight crunch, making me cringe, and yet I understand there's almost no chance I'm going to get by without being discovered. Needless to say there's adrenaline pumping through my veins. But there's also an odd calmness to the encounter, things moving slowly enough to allow me the satisfaction of knowing that I'm giving this my best shot. If he moves toward me my plan is to try to yell him away, and if that doesn't work prepare to unload the pepper spray. And if that doesn't work—well, I don't really have a plan for that, though dropping into fetal position is, in truth, the last ditch, if somewhat pathetic alternative. And then he looks up. Spots me right away. And on locking eyes he hesitates only a split second, then turns his beautiful, plump self on a dime—his rolls of fat shuddering with the sudden movement—and runs off into the woods without a snort or grunt. I clutch the pepper spray for a while, keep looking behind me as I make my way down the trail to make sure I'm not being followed. Except for the squawking of ravens and Clark's nutcrackers, the occasional buzz of a chickadee, all is quiet.

While I'm inclined to take the number of bears seen by outfitters with a grain of salt (remember the 130-member Delta wolf pack), there's no question that there are lots of them roaming the Teton Wilderness. Cavan Fitzsimmons alone will see 18 different grizzlies on his hunting patrols this year, including sows with triplets, all of them in good shape. In 1993, the U.S. Fish and Wildlife Service established three basic recovery goals to be achieved before the grizzly could be removed from the threatened species list, where they landed amid enormous controversy in the summer of 1975. The first goal calls for establishing 15 adult females with cubs of the year for six years on average, both inside the recovery zone and within a ten-mile area immediately surrounding it. The second goal is to have 16 out of 18 Bear Management Units occupied by females with young, again over a six-year period. The final target calls for human-caused bear mortality in any two consecutive years to be no more than 4 percent of the current population; furthermore, no more than 30 percent of those mortalities can be females. The bears of the Yellowstone ecosystem have met all those parameters in each of four years from 1998 through 2001, and they seem likely to meet them again this year. In addition to these objectives, actual delisting requires the states of Montana, Wyoming, and Idaho to have management plans in place to ensure proper monitoring and management of both the bears and their habitat.

In such a conservative region of the country, where the federal government is about as popular as RuPaul, there's great suspicion that way too many bureaucrats have jobs wrapped up in the grizzly to ever let it go. "If those biologists would come and spend three weeks with an outfitter," one guide told me, commenting on the great number of bears in the area, "they'd say holy shit. Instead they sit in their offices with their computers and let the problems keep going." But even acknowledging that numbers are good, even very good, there are issues related to resources that, when taken together, give pause to even the most optimistic bear pundit. For starters, not only have the all-important whitebark pine nuts been hard to come by because of drought, but a great many of those trees—over 80 percent—are likely to be lost over the next ten years to blister rust. They may never come back, in large part because of warming climate conditions; even if they do it could take a good 80 or even 100 years to produce healthy crops of nuts. At the same time another important food source, spawning cutthroat trout, have declined in some streams by as much as 50 percent. Add to this increasing bear conflicts with hunters—which of course often leads to increased mortality—as well as potential threats to habitat from numerous energy development schemes, and what seems like a rock-solid population of grizzlies today could crumble tomorrow.

As I reach the lower stretches of Atlantic Creek a curtain of lodgepole pine falls away to reveal a glorious view north through the Thorofare—in all some 20 miles of meadow lit by the setting sun, braced on the east by Hawks Rest and The Trident and Turret Mountain, on the west by Two Ocean Plateau. Stopping to savor the view, I recall something Kayla once said about this place, that as crazy as it is on any given summer day, what with gun-toting outfitters and dudes muscling through some B-movie version of the Wild West, it's still a miracle the place was never developed. That highways or railroads were never punched across this flat, idyllic terrain, that the meadows aren't lying dead and forgotten under golf courses and condominiums, fast-food restaurants and trinket shops and motels. Even in Yellowstone Park, there were for years aggressive plans for damming both Yellowstone Lake and the Bechler River; here in the Thorofare, the Army got downright snotty during the 1940s trying to push through a landing field.

On the other hand, in 1918 this entire area—including the headwaters of the Yellowstone River and Thorofare Creek, all the way south to the Buffalo Fork—barely missed being included in an expansion of Yellowstone National Park. It was part of a "greater Yellowstone" movement that had been brewing in fits and starts since General Sheridan first suggested doubling the size of the park in 1882 to better protect its game. "Give her Greater Yellowstone," as Emerson Hough wrote in the *Saturday Evening Post* in 1917, "and she will inevitably become Greater Wyoming." Nor was such effort merely the work of outsiders. It was none other than Wyoming's lone congressman, Frank Mondell, who introduced the 1918 extension plan into the House of Representatives, while a similar measure was proposed to the

Senate by Wyoming Senator John Kendrick. Both measures were endorsed by Governor Carey. Had the proposal not been too near the bottom of the Senate calendar to receive a hearing, it would've passed easily in that same year.

Yet by the time another year came and went, not only had the Jackson Hole Livestock Association rallied their troops against the measure, but also, and perhaps even more significantly, a powerful Easterner and big-game hunter named I. H. Larom, who rattled the cages of state legislators in the name of hunting, ultimately convincing them to oppose the plan. A more modest extension—though still protecting the headwaters of the Yellowstone—was proposed a decade later, tied to a bill creating Grand Teton National Park. This too had powerful support both in Wyoming as well as nationally, including that of President Calvin Coolidge. However, there was still wrangling over issues related to the Yellowstone expansion, which in the end led legislators to split off the bill that would create Grand Teton National Park. The boundary extension that finally passed in 1929 added 159 square miles to Yellowstone, while at the same time transferred 81 square miles of existing parkland to the national forests. This time, though, the headwaters of both Thorofare Creek and Yellowstone River, which had been part of every extension effort of the past, were removed altogether—an eleventh-hour concession to appease irate outfitters in Cody. "It was absolutely impossible to get this country included," wrote National Park Service Director Horace Albright. "So I decided to take at this time what we could get."

There's a profound quiet to the days following my farewell to LaVoy. The one remaining horse camp, a friendly group from Salt Lake City who's been coming to Hawks Rest for a dozen years, pulls the pickets on Labor Day, leaving me alone in that brief, beautiful pause before the guns of autumn. It's as if the wildlife too is immediately aware of the shift. Shortly after dawn on September 3, at that time of day when the river bottom is still wrapped in ribbons of fog, while building a fire in the cookstove, I hear the unmistakable howl of a wolf. Dropping my kindling and running out to the porch, I listen as there comes three or four minutes of soulful calling by a single animal not a thousand yards away, somewhere near the south shore of Bridger Lake. Much like the thunder of summer storms, the sound bounces off the steep cliffs at the base of Two Ocean Plateau then crosses the valley to ricochet off Hawks Rest. An acoustic marvel, lending a timbre that strengthens the already stirring qualities of the song. Both those who despise and those who delight in wolves often describe their howls as something that makes the hair on the backs of their necks stand on end. That's never happened to me. Whether in chorus or alone, wolf howling brings to mind something sad but rich, the blues of the world, as if some ancient pain was being exorcised through their upturned muzzles. Fifteen minutes later, I spot two young black wolves just beyond the pasture fence trotting north, hugging a line of willows on their way toward Bridger Lake. The same wailing that to me seems like Billie Holiday at her most pained is perhaps to them more the equivalent of a mother standing on the back stoop, calling her wandering kids home for supper.

There's also in these early days of September a conspicuous increase in animals right around the cabin; one chipmunk in particular peers in the west window every morning and every night, pawing at the glass, trying to figure a way in. Likewise, the woods behind me are full of red squirrels cutting hundreds of cones from Douglas-fir and spruce trees, which either drop to the ground with a considerable thud or else bounce off fallen logs, leaving me on some days feeling like I'm living on the 200-yard line of a driving range. For most of this morning six mule deer have been hanging close—three does and three fawns—standing not a dozen feet from the porch, staring through the screen door between bites of grass. Eventually they make their way under the top rail of the fence and mosey down to the pasture, then drift away.

At night I find myself restless with images of foul-tempered grizzlies. Not just during late trips to the outhouse, but sometimes even in the cabin, where my bunk squats in the same corner that 60 years ago was thoroughly dismantled by a crazed bear. The Park Service has been issuing press releases about an increase in maulings, saying the danger is up because of another lousy whitebark pine nut crop. Besides all that, by the time I leave here it'll be well into the hunting season. What if Bob Jackson is right, that salting and quick quartering in the northern reaches of the Teton Wilderness is pulling touchy bears across the southern boundary of the park to feed on elk carcasses? My route out, meant to trace one of the longest elk migrations in the Rockies, will follow exactly that line.

I'M WRITING THIS from the porch, sitting on an overturned aluminum horse pannier, my back against the rail and my face to the sun. The river, having swelled somewhat with last week's rains, has released its extra cargo and is again back to a quiet set of meanders. At times, for no apparent reason, the rapids just below the bridge become suddenly audible, drifting up to the cabin in a loud whisper, only to disappear a few seconds later. Tied to the lower hitching rail are three mules, stomping and snorting—part of a pack string left behind by Cavan and his partner Erin, who right now are up Thorofare Creek checking possible salting sites. Jack Hatch and his buddy Bill, meanwhile, along with Dann Harvey from the Wyoming Wilderness Academy, are cruising around the southern reaches of the park looking for wolves.

Last night there were six of us sleeping in the cabin, five in the main room and Jack on the lower bunk in the tack room. Bill snores like crazy, making my next to last night here seem like a slumber party in a woodshop. With morning came another great salon, this time led by horse genius Jack Hatch, the guy who breaks wild mustangs for the Forest Service. "Seems like most people are overwhelmed by machines," he told us over coffee brewed so thick a little dog couldn't make a track in it. "And what those machines have done is to make us lose our intuitive abilities." He told us that ever since he can remember he's wanted to devote his life to doing simple things really well. By simple, he means intuitive. Which is why he likes working with horses. "Horses are like people in this way," he explained. "They hunger for freedom. A horse will always seek out that space where he's most free from controlling influences." Which sounds a lot like what LaVoy was saying about that grizzly bear we saw along the Lamar, the one that turned and ran from us like the wind—maybe for no other reason than to protect his space.

On the day of my departure, I leave not an empty, quiet cabin, but one thick with the smell of coffee and oatmeal. Cavan

and Erin are getting ready for a long trek up the Yellowstone, Jack
and Bill are off to Blackrock to gentle some troubled mustangs,
Dann will head to Laramie, to Cathedral Home, to square
dance with troubled kids. The weather is warm so the elk are
still high on the tundra, or slightly below, hidden in scattered curtains of unburned timber. Game warden Gary Brown and his
daughter pass me at Open Creek, bringing in supplies to the
Game and Fish cabin. He talks of the migration to come here in
the Thorofare Creek drainage around the third week in October,
elk moving east by the hundreds, by the thousands, the place
looking like a frozen Serengeti. Indeed, I've decided to walk out
Thorofare Creek, then up Bruin Creek, and down Fall Creek
entirely because of this movement—one of the largest, most dramatic migrations anywhere in the Rockies. Of course I'm well
ahead of the elk, but then the degree of weather needed to
prompt my leaving is far less than what's needed to prompt theirs.
Even now there could come snow, a foot or two in a matter of
hours, blanketing the tundra separating this drainage from that
of the South Fork of the Shoshone. With that in mind I find
myself turning back often to the west, watching for the kinds of
clouds that signal snow. But there's only rain threatening, and
by evening the sky clears and temperatures drop to around 20
degrees, coating the tent fly with a sheet of ice.

The final outpost before leaving the main trail is Gary
Fales' camp, some 16 miles from Hawks Rest, perched at the edge
of a glorious run of meadow on the upper reaches of Thorofare
Creek. On my arrival the camp is bustling, guides rolling hides
and piling four- and six-point antler racks, putting things in
order for tomorrow's long ride out to Cody. Seven out of 11
hunters have taken animals, and there's a good chance others will

score before nightfall. Two of the clients—Pete from Georgia and Dan from Pennsylvania—stand in their cowboy hats leaning on a hitching rail, chewing on stems of grass. Both seem eager to talk, especially about grizzlies.

"When's the last time you saw a bear?" Dan wants to know, and seems surprised when I tell him it's been a week. "We've got them all over, coming into camp almost every night." He tells me that yesterday one of the group took a nice bull; by the time they went back for the pack string and returned, maybe three hours, a grizzly had buried the carcass and was lying on it. "One of the guides had to plug birdshot into a big sow with a 12-gauge just to run it off," Pete says with a vacant look. "It was either that, or he would've had to kill it." In three weeks it'll be bullets instead of birdshot, as a troublesome bear will wander into this same camp one too many times, end up meeting his maker here in the upper meadows of Thorofare Creek. In all it reminds me of an entry made in the logbook of the Hawks Rest cabin 20 years ago by Teton Wilderness ranger Gordon Reese: "We've had no bear issues. Wet year and lead poisoning have alleviated the problem."

The guides within earshot stay quiet, but from the looks on their faces it's clear they're not happy about the loose talk, especially the part about firing birdshot into a bear with a 12-gauge. I've got a backpack on, after all—and boots with Vibram soles—which makes me not the sort of person to chew with about grizzly control. When I ask one of them the best way to move overland up Bruin Creek to the divide, he says only to stick to the bottom. Which is completely different from the advice I got from John Winter's son, who two weeks ago assured me that the best route would be along the high slopes to the north. You'd think after all these years I would've learned. While most guides wouldn't hesitate to offer help to someone who really needed it, bullshitting backpackers is a favorite pastime—either by giving wrong directions or, more common still, telling you about the big grizzly waiting for you just around the corner.

Stupidly I stick to the bottom, and a mile up the creek find myself in the bowels of a pinched canyon some 200 feet deep, water flowing wall to wall. It takes some serious searching to find a way up and out, and in the end I'm left climbing a narrow, precipitous slot, sending bowling ball–size rocks thundering into the chasm below. In reality, the hunting trail doesn't actually hit the stream for several miles, losing itself in willow patches and tumbles of downfall, in thickets so dense there's nothing to do but keep calling to the bears and hoping for the best.

After a long steady climb the path finally reaches broken forest—long sprawls of whitebark pine, more than half of them dead or dying from blister rust. From a distance, their bulbous canopies, the color now a mix of avocado and rust, make them look like deciduous trees fading under the weight of autumn. By midafternoon I've reached the tundra, a wind-tossed jumble of ridges more than 11,000 feet high, the center line forming the backbone of the Absaroka divide. There are regular highways beaten into the vegetation from the passing of thousands of elk, most of them tumbling over the lip of the divide into Fall Creek, then making for the South Fork of the Shoshone and the steep shoulders of Needle Mountain. Once again I grow dizzy trying to sort it all out—the gentle lilt of Thorofare Plateau to the west, Deer Creek Pass and Rampart Peak to the north, and well to the east, sage-covered plains along the lower South Fork of the Shoshone. Beyond that Cody, and the end of the wild.

Just a few hours from now, almost in the very spot where I'm standing, a gripping event will happen that I won't hear about until my return to civilization. A guide from Gary Fales' camp by the name of Mike Potas is on his way here with a hunting client, tracking elk. On reaching this slice of the divide a sow grizzly bear will surprise him from behind, taking hold of his thigh and shaking him like a rag doll, finally tossing him down the side of the mountain, bruised and bleeding. Talking with him later this fall, I'll mention that the whole thing sounds about as scary as it gets. "Not really," he'll tell me. "Didn't have enough time to be scared." Forest Service ranger Cavan Fitzsimmons will hear the report over the radio later today, figure it's me.

At the same time Mike Potas is slam dancing with grizzlies, I'm tripping down the crumbling soil of Fall Creek, dropping 5,000 feet in about five miles. If the hiking is lousy, the sightseeing is anything but: the creek a series of nearly vertical drops broken by icy blue-green pools. The south wall of the canyon is hung with thin waterfalls dropping off the lips of volcanic ledges, while on the north side the streams are more substantial, rocketing off stony chutes, launching themselves into space like kids jumping off their swings. By the last two miles, what trail there is has braided and disintegrated under washouts and slides, making the descent an utterly freelance affair. Looking at my maps—I'm traveling with topos that have 80-foot contour intervals instead of 40, which I've sworn many times not to do—it's hard to tell whether or not I can drop directly out of this drainage into the South Fork of the Shoshone, or if I should instead head upstream and look for a better route. I stand beside a mighty plunge of Fall Creek for ten minutes or so, staring down through a thick curtain of timber, trying to gauge whether the

202 | Hawks Rest

trees descend all the way into the South Fork, which, if they do, could give me some measure of purchase. I've got a bad feeling about it, though, and so in the end decide to cross the creek in my sandals just above the falls, crawl out the other side, and begin paralleling the South Fork drainage, looking for another way down. It takes a good half mile of rough hiking to find it, and even then reaching the valley is a slippery affair.

It's close to five o'clock when I finally set up camp on the far side of the South Fork, well above the water in a small cluster of lodgepole. Being my last night in the wilds I decide to build a fire, stare into the flames and try to imagine what it will be like to have all this behind me. Given the hunting season is on I figured on see-ing plenty of horse traffic, but all is quiet—at least until around 6:30, when a lone backpacker from Cody shows up. Considering the lack of campsites in the immediate area, I'm happy to share this one with him, and we sit on logs next to the fire and talk for three hours before we even find out each other's name. Steve says he tried hard to find someone to come with him on this three-day trek, with no luck. "Anymore people are either too busy or too out of shape," he explains. So he goes alone, though he'd rather not.

During the summer Steve's a rafting guide on the Shoshone. Rather than telling me what's great about that job, though, he talks instead about the bizarre questions he keeps getting from the guests. The one that confounds him the most, which he says he hears a good half-dozen times a week, is whether or not the raft ends up at the same place the crew puts it in. As if the river flowed in a big loop. "I used to find that really funny," he says quietly. "But now it seems scary. I mean we're talking about a lot of otherwise intelligent people, who have absolutely no con-cept of the basic laws that drive the world. Things like gravity."

When I rise to leave the next morning, Steve's still sacked out, so I leave a piece of paper with my address on it and head downstream, beginning the final walk of the season. When I reach a point opposite Fall Creek, it becomes abundantly clear that I made the right choice yesterday. That steep curtain of conifers at the lip of the falls would've led in no time to a hundred-foot cliff. Even if I made it down—and the chances of that are slim to none—at the base of the falls the river runs through the canyon wall to wall. My insane descent would've been followed by a long trudge downstream on slippery rocks in knee-deep ice water; two miles of that before reaching a steep slot in the canyon where I could've at last climbed up several hundred feet to the trail.

Instead, I'm on a beautiful stretch of pathway on a cliff edge high above the river, trying to go slow—especially since it will be hours before Jane arrives at the trailhead—a couple times parking myself in an open meadow just to take it all in, burn the day into memory so I can reach for it when life gets screwy in the months ahead. The west wall of the canyon is stunning, a canto to erosion. A thousand feet up are a good half dozen pinched ravines, where, after every heavy rain, streams of water thunder into magnificent falls. Just below each narrowed slot, at those places where the water is funneled before leaping into oblivion, are staggering piles of gravel some 400 or 500 feet high. The highlands, in other words, are being turned into scree, which in turn is being broken into sand and then washed into the river. The world of mountains is turning yet again into a land of plains.

CHAPTER TEN

THE END CAME IN EARLY EVENING, UNDER a warm blue September sky. I was euphoric for several weeks, simmering in that in-between time when I was out of the wilderness but not completely out, freshly reunited with friends and loved ones but not yet overwhelmed by daily demands. A time for pondering what environmentalist Sigurd Olson said was the final measure of the worth of wrapping yourself in wildness in the first place. You can't stay back there, he cautioned, because that's not where the people are. Going to nature was in truth an exercise in renewal, a "balm for the tensions of the world": "Wilderness to the people of America is a spiritual necessity, an antidote to the high pressure of modern life, a means of regaining serenity and equilibrium.... They go to the wilderness for the good of their souls."

It's a tall order. I left the song and shadow of Hawks Rest and came back to a world rife with fear, full of corporate scandals,

and a government once again eager for war. It's at times a struggle to hang on to the beauty, to not dishonor it by waking up
on sour mornings and questioning if any of it was real. I saw
Kayla in early October in Jackson, and, on that day at least, she
too was at wit's end, promising in a huff that if things didn't get
better on the political scene she'd load up her pack and walk
back into the Thorofare and disappear for good. She won't, of
course, because deep inside it's not her nature to drop out
entirely. Even in the wilds she needed people to listen to her
story, to acknowledge the wisdom she's gained by giving leash
to that brilliant and demanding dream that's been tugging at her
for 20 years.

Besides, it's not like the Teton Wilderness wasn't without
madness of its own. In truth, wild places have always engen-
dered crass lawlessness as easily as sensitivity, sparking
dunderheaded arrogance in addition to gratitude and inspiration. The same place that's proven such a magnet to the likes
of Kayla Michael and Bob Jackson, to the kids of the Wyoming
Wilderness Academy, is also a powerful draw for a whole host
of dropouts and zealots. In a way, to expect anything less is to
diminish the power of the wilds. Aggression and grace, fury and
birth, life and death are all played out in such places, and one
plucks only the inspiring parts at the risk of reducing the land
to flatness.

Not that I wasn't at various times appalled by the abusive,
near warlord mentality of the Thorofare. I can barely imagine
a more hypocritical stance than the one common there that
curses the government, rails against wolves and grizzly bears, all
the while squeezing dollars out of lands that would never have
been available for outfitting in the first place had a great many

devoted conservationists not pushed hard for their protection.
The hunter, as Theodore Roosevelt defined him, a man who
fights for the integrity of both his prey and the land that sustained
it, is being too often overwhelmed by men concerned mostly with
playing dress up and shooting guns. More irritating still is the
fact that such rhetoric was so often wrapped in the flag. Thereby
reducing one of the great bedrocks of patriotism—the celebration
of unfettered land, so common in early America—into a profane
demand for the right to despoil it.

Yet there are disturbing signs on the other side of the fence
as well. While visiting as a guest lecturer recently at one of the
nation's foremost political science departments, I happened to
ask a leading scholar why she happened to care about greater
Yellowstone. She was silent for a minute, thinking hard, then with
a look of great satisfaction told me that it was because the place
"has exceptional cultural cachet." Meanwhile, it's hard to find a
single resource manager who isn't dismayed by how visitors are
increasingly behaving around wildlife, as if greater Yellowstone
is Disney World with thermal features. There are cell phone rescues by the dozens of people who simply grow tired on the trail
and perceptions of wildlife that seem innocent to the point of
being evil. "There's a generation of people now so removed from
the outdoors that they don't have a clue," says biologist Kerry
Gunther. "People think nothing of walking right up to within 20
yards of a 400-pound grizzly."

At the same time has come a willingness to curse ranchers
and others of the rural West at every turn. On the most pragmatic
level, such attitudes show a terrible ignorance of the fact that elk
and certain other wildlife are absolutely dependent on private
ranchlands (unlike deer, they will not cozy up to subdivisions),

and that if you lose the elk you begin to lose wolves, not to mention grizzlies, coyotes, badgers, and eagles. Furthermore, to grouse about eliminating wolves that develop a taste for livestock, while at the same time being perfectly willing to cover the winter range of their prey base with trophy homes and condominiums is no less arrogant—and many times more consequential—than anything being done by a given lunatic in the Thorofare. Beyond even that, though, the willingness to unravel peoples' lives without mercy, destroy what are, at least on good days, sustainable pursuits—cooking up visions of nature based not on community in the broadest, most diverse sense, but on elitist dogma—is a kind of blood sport all its own. One that reduces nature from a living force to the status of a token.

I went to the Thorofare to gauge the state of nature in the most remote place in the lower 48. On first glance it seems remarkably intact. No doubt wolves will howl and bears will scratch yampa and biscuit-root from the meadows along the upper Yellowstone for years to come. On any given summer afternoon there will be soaring overhead everything from sandhill cranes to Swainson's hawks, eagles to marsh hawks, pelicans to peregrine falcons. Despite the growing knot of humanity sprawling southward from the shores of Bridger Lake, it will still be possible to wander off onto windswept ridges or hidden vales swimming with quietude. Yet even a sprawl of wildness as grand and unfettered as this one cannot survive forever a culture increasingly hard-bitten and self-absorbed. One that on many days seems willing to trade a heritage of conservation, with its requisites of empathy and affinity, for mere adjudication. A society in which good science becomes less important than good press releases, where on most days the battle seems less about guaranteeing an actual future than securing an imagined past. Beyond the creatures it plays host to, the Thorofare serves an enormous range of human hungers. Perhaps one day those who depend on it will look around at the palette of life there and realize that such abundance owes less to survival of the fittest than it does to the creative potential of diversity—that he who would dominate the system is sewing the seeds of his own destruction.

AFTER WE SPLIT UP at Parting of the Waters, LaVoy walked 21 miles to the Turpin Meadow Trailhead in six hours. Finally home again in late September, his boots had barely cooled before he was out roaming again, this time through the canyons of southern Utah. Bob Jackson was by October back in Iowa raising buffalo. On January 22, 2003, he got a call from Lake sub-district ranger Michael Keeter, informing him that his job at Thorofare had been changed from seasonal work to a career conditional position, which means the slot will be filled by someone with more law enforcement credentials. (A curious turn of events, given how many Yellowstone officials told Frank Deluka that nothing of consequence was going on in the Thorofare.) Jackson was told he'd have the choice of either quitting altogether, or else have his name placed in a pool of employees available to other supervisors, where as likely as not he'd end up babysitting an entrance gate. Ironically, the justification for this change can be found in a homeland security measure launched in part by Jackson's political ally, Iowa Senator Chuck Grassley who, after the September 11 terrorist attacks, called for stronger law enforcement throughout the Department of Interior. Despite the bleak picture, Bob's faithful supporter, the group Public Employees for Environmental Responsibility, plans to intervene yet again. "We got him back in there the past two years," says Dan Meyer. "My prediction is that we'll get him back again."

Some of the outfitters Bob routinely spars with were again spotted hunting over salts; another guide was caught poaching in the park. A worker at a hunting camp on upper Thorofare Creek was playing drinking games, got three sheets to the wind one night and accidentally killed himself with a pistol in the cook tent. Teton Wilderness manager Rob St. John has been furiously writing grant proposals, trying to gather enough money to do even basic trail work in the coming year. By mid-November several big snows had fallen, leaving no one in the Thorofare with the possible exception of that one steely true believer, the illegal outfitter who each year roams that wild country, hunting for God.

In the weeks following my departure the bears were out in force. Even moose sightings were way up, poking yet another hole in the claims of those who say wolves are wiping them out. And speaking of wolves, Wyoming launched yet another harebrained management plan, this one calling for the animals to be treated as a game species in the wilderness and as predators elsewhere. Given that such a proposal does nothing to assure stable wolf populations in the future—in Wyoming, after all, predators can be pretty much shot on sight—it was dead before it hit the ground, delaying even further that time when the animal can be removed from the endangered species list. Meanwhile, in Wyoming's Fremont County, commissioners voted 3-2 to entertain a request by legendary property-rights fanatic Rudy Stanko to kill wolves on his grazing leases in the Bridger-Teton National Forest. "I've already had 15 verified wolf kills and 11 bear kills and the wolves killed all my cow dogs in our camp last week," Stanko told the commission, in a tale that makes the wolf in Little Red Riding Hood look like the Taco Bell chihuahua. "These wolves are having several litters of pups a year and I'm here to tell you fellows they are on the move." When it's all said and done, Stanko may well do as he pleases, with or without blessings from the commissioners, as he's often claimed the entire Endangered Species Act is unconstitutional.

The cutthroat trout have long since moved back to Yellowstone Lake, the elk to winter range—some moving along the east side of the Snake River to Jackson, others to the Greybull River. The Delta pack has been moving up and down the frozen edges of the Yellowstone River and Thorofare Creek, their steps barely a whisper in the driven snow. The four pups that seemed like such a chore back in July are now an asset, traveling and hunting with the pack, and when necessary, defending territory. In January, biologists tried again to radio collar several members of the group, but this time found them hunkered down in the Teton Wilderness, where helicopter operations are prohibited.

As for me, home is home again. Through the south-facing window above my desk I can see the lumpy ridges of Mount Maurice, frozen fast against the south horizon, stung by the best early winter we've had in years. Now and then a certain cow moose ambles by the kitchen, stopping to cast a longing look at the plants growing on the windowsill; overhead ravens croak and wheel in the sky, black shadows in a world of white.

Midway up the mountain, in a half dozen scrapes of soil and tumbled clefts of granite, sow bears and their cubs sleep like worn-out children. Beyond these and well out of view, the land jumps 2,000 feet to become another world—two miles high and locked in numbing winds, snow piled into ten-foot drifts, rock splintering by the yard as ice freezes and thaws in fissures of granite.

The greater Yellowstone of lore. Out of sight, but almost never out of mind.

CHRONOLOGY OF EVENTS

1872   Yellowstone National Park established
1900   Lacey Act passed (first federal wildlife protection law);
       last amended in 1981
1908   Teton National Forest designated
1905   Teton Game Preserve established
1912   National Elk Refuge established
1916   Bridger National Forest designated
1929   Grand Teton National Park established
1964   Wilderness Act passed
1964   Teton Wilderness congressionally designated a wilderness
       area within Teton National Forest
1973   Endangered Species Act passed
1973   Bridger and Teton National Forests combined
1975   Final listing (threatened) of grizzly bear on Endangered
       Species List
1976   Final listing (endangered) of gray wolf on Endangered
       Species List

1988   More than 1.6 million acres burned in Yellowstone
       National Park and surrounding forests
1991   Salting prohibited in Teton Wilderness
1995   First reintroduction of gray wolves to greater Yellowstone
2001   Wyoming state law prohibits the hunting of big game ani-
       mals over bait (including salt) placed outside of normal
       agricultural practices

ACKNOWLEDGMENTS

A SPECIAL THANKS to the staunch and spirited trail crews of the Bridger-Teton National Forest, to manager Rob St. John, and forest historian James Schoen. Thanks also to grizzly biologists Chuck Schwartz and Kerry Gunther, Yellowstone National Park wolf project director Doug Smith, park historian Lee Whittlesey, and Wyoming Game and Fish warden Tim Fagan. My gratitude as well to that virtuoso of researchers, Judy McHale, to my agent, Gordon Kato, and to National Geographic editors Jane Sunderland and Elizabeth Newhouse. Finally, warm thanks for the nourishment afforded by those indomitable women of Café Regis—Jane, Martha, and Sharon.

ABOUT THE AUTHOR

*G*ARY FERGUSON, a former Forest Service ranger, has written more than a dozen books on nature and science. His 1997 book, *The Sylvan Path: A Journey through America's Forests,* won the Lowell Thomas Award for best nature writing. *Spirits of the Wild: The World's Great Nature Myths* was selected by the New York City Public Library as one of the best books of 1996. Ferguson's essays can be heard on National Public Radio. He and his wife, Jane, live in south-central Montana.

COLOPHON

𝒯HIS BOOK was set in Berthold Baskerville Book, redesigned in 1980 by Günter Gerhard Lange and based upon the original design of John Baskerville (1752-1757). The drop caps are set in P22 Dearest Script, designed by Christina Torre and inspired by hand-written characters found in a 19th-century German book. The title type is P22 Vincent, based upon the handwriting of Vincent van Gogh.

917.8752 Ferguson, Gary,
FER   1956-

      Hawks rest.

$15.00